GEORGE AND LOUISE SPINDLER
Stanford University

RESEARCH DESIGN IN ANTHROPOLOGY:
PARADIGMS AND PRAGMATICS
IN THE TESTING OF HYPOTHESES

RESEARCH DESIGN IN ANTHROPOLOGY

Paradigms and Pragmatics in the Testing of Hypotheses

JOHN A. BRIM
Rutgers, The State University

DAVID H. SPAIN
The University of Washington

HOLT, RINEHART AND WINSTON
New York   Chicago   San Francisco   Atlanta
Dallas   Montreal   Toronto   London   Sydney

" . . . anthropology, with its predilection
for studying small-scale societies largely without
recent, more technical methods,
has become *relatively* less prominent."

Talcott Parsons
(1966:112)

For: Ronald Cohen
Roy D'Andrade
Raoul Naroll
A. Kimball Romney
George Spindler

—contemporary pioneers
in anthropological method,
and our exacting mentors.

Library of Congress Cataloging in Publication Data

Brim, John A.
    Research design in anthropology.

    (Studies in anthropological method)
    Bibliography: p. 112
    1. Anthropology—Methodology. 2. Anthropological
research. I. Spain, David H., joint author.
II. Title. III. Series.
GN33.B73   301.2'07'2   73-8837

ISBN: 0-03-011451-9

Foreword

ABOUT THE SERIES
Anthropology has been, since the turn of the century, a significant influence shaping Western thought. It has brought into proper perspective the position of our culture as one of many and has challenged universalistic and absolutistic assumptions and beliefs about the proper condition of man. Anthropology has been able to make this contribution mainly through its descriptive analyses of non-Western ways of life. Only in the last decades of its comparatively short existence as a science have anthropologists developed systematic theories about human behavior in its transcultural dimensions, and only very recently have anthropological techniques of data collection and analysis become explicit and in some instances replicable.

Teachers of anthropology have been handicapped by the lack of clear, authoritative statements of how anthropologists collect and analyze relevant data. The results of fieldwork are available in the ethnographies and they can be used to demonstrate cultural diversity and integration, social control, religious behavior, marriage customs, and the like, but clear, systematic statements about how the facts are gathered and interpreted are rare in the literature readily available to students. Without this information the alert reader of anthropological literature is left uninformed about the process of our science, knowing only of the results. This is an unsatisfying state of affairs for both the student and the instructor.

The series is designed to help solve this problem. Each study in the series focuses upon manageable dimensions of modern anthropological methodology. Each one demonstrates significant aspects of the processes of gathering, ordering, and interpreting data. Some are highly selected dimensions of methodology. Others are concerned with the whole range of experience involved in studying a total society. These studies are written by professional anthropologists who have done fieldwork and have made significant contributions to the science of man and his works. In them the authors explain how they go about this work, and to what end. We think they will be helpful to students who want to know what processes of inquiry and ordering stand behind the formal, published results of anthropology.

ABOUT THE AUTHORS

John Brim is assistant professor of anthropology at Livingston College of Rutgers University. He did fieldwork in the New Territories of Hong Kong in 1967–1969 and received his Ph.D. in anthropology from Stanford University in 1970. His area of specialization is psychological anthropology.

David H. Spain teaches anthropology at the University of Washington. He has done fieldwork in Nigeria among the Kanuri in 1965 and in 1966–1967. He holds the Ph.D. in anthropology from Northwestern University. He is a co-author of

Tradition and Identity in Changing Africa (published by Harper and Row) and a co-editor of *Survey Research in Africa: Its Applications and Limits* (published by Northwestern University Press). His interests are primarily in the fields of culture and personality, and sociocultural change.

ABOUT THE BOOK

John Brim and David Spain have discussed in this book four common research paradigms. A paradigm is the element of the design that structures or patterns the measurement of variables. Specifically they discuss the pretest-posttest, the static-group-comparison, the nonequivalent-control-group, and the control-group paradigms. They have laid out their discussion of these paradigms, which in the larger sense might be called stratagems of research, in such a way that the reader can identify common sources of error by anticipating the errors to which a given research design may be subject. It may be possible to avoid them, or if it is not possible to avoid them—as it frequently is not—at least their effects may be reduced. Brim and Spain do not make excessive claims for any of the research designs they discuss. They take into consideration the peculiar difficulties of the anthropological situation and agree that it is often not possible to confirm hypotheses but conclude that researchers may at least effectively probe them.

The authors are mindful of the diversity of opinion among anthropologists concerning the utility of research designs such as those described in this book. Most of us have not been as rigorous in our designing or execution of research as Brim and Spain would have us be. The personal and humanistic dimensions loom so large that often the demands placed upon one by scientifically acceptable research design seem impossibly burdensome or even irrelevant. It may well be that in the long run of human affairs the scientific side of anthropology will prove to be less important than the humanistic. Anthropology has already contributed significantly to the stream of consciousness that is interpenetrating knowledgeable minds in all the cultures of the world, just as did psychoanalysis only yesterday and Aristotelian logic not too long before that. Seen from this point of view, the task of the anthropologist is primarily to apply a trained mind to the observation and analysis of behaviors in cultural settings other than his or her own—to epitomize, to characterize, to communicate the meaning of a way of life across cultural boundaries. Anthropology in this tradition is careful observation and careful analysis, but it is also humanistic and even poetic. Perhaps there is no common meeting ground between this kind of anthropology and the kind so clearly described and defended in this book by Brim and Spain.

This is, however, probably not really the case. Both kinds of anthropology have the common purpose of explaining behavior, just as do all of the social sciences and their subdivisions. The problem is perhaps one of the unit of explanation. Anthropologists began with assortments of esoterica—museum pieces, the stories of travelers, myths about myths. The culture concept rose to supremacy in anthropological thinking as a way of bringing together all the bits and pieces or the "shreds and tatters," as the saying goes. The culture concept gave anthropologists a way of feeling that they knew what the boundaries of explanation were. Culture was (and still is) seen as a working system of interrelated parts. This concept, too, has been superseded in some quarters by other approaches. The tendency has been to break the master concept into smaller, more manageable, pieces but not those like the ones in the collection of "shreds and tatters." Ethnoscience and ethnosemantics, for example, have attempted to reduce the level of description to manageable, highly specific, more or less replicative units, but at the same time ecologists and ethologists are telling us that the culture concept is too limited. The unit of explanation must not be man's behavior as a whole or even man as a whole, but rather man's adaptation in a total environment only part of which is man-made. The culture concept permitted us to become relativistic in our judgment of the interrelationship of the working parts in the whole. Ecology and ethology call upon us to view cultural systems as more or less effective working adaptations to a total life and life-support system that is a stern judge of the dysfunctional.

It is not at all unhealthy for the state of our discipline that there are different kinds of attempts to reach a common goal. The methods and logic set forth in this book will produce useful results if applied rigorously. The task of explaining what those results mean to the survival of humankind on this planet is another kind of task and one that we, as anthropologists, may never succeed in doing very well.

Whatever the relevance of these large considerations, every student of anthropology would do well to study this volume carefully and understand what it is saying. If one chooses not to apply as rigorous a research methodology as is possible under whatever conditions obtain, then he or she should be prepared to defend this choice.

GEORGE AND LOUISE SPINDLER
General Editors
Stanford, 1973

ACKNOWLEDGMENTS

In writing this book, we incurred debts to numerous individuals which we wish to acknowledge here. First, as our dedication indicates, we acknowledge with pleasure our debts to our mentors at Stanford and Northwestern Universities; it is they who provided the principal stimulus for this book. Second, and quite simply, we recognize the unending generosity of our wives, Gloria and Cathie. We value their support more than words can say. Third, we acknowledge our colleagues and friends whose opinions, put forth in the best spirit of an eclectic anthropology, have provided us with points and counterpoints in our thinking. We have gained much from these encounters. Finally, we recognize our rather large debt to those of our students who read and commented upon various portions of the manuscript, adding much to it in the process. Notable among these have been Albert and Margaret Hollenbeck and Joan Carol Golston.

In writing this book, we became aware anew that being a critic is even more difficult when one is also a performer. We also became aware, in part because of our field experiences, that doing in fact what one knows should be done in theory may often be extremely difficult. Indeed, our decision to discuss both paradigms and pragmatics reflects this. But we have written this book in the conviction that anthropologists who improve the design of their hypothesis testing research will be amply rewarded for their efforts.

J. A. B.
D. H. S.

Contents

Foreword   *iii*

1. INTRODUCTION   *1*
    Theories and the Origin of Hypotheses   *2*
    Organization and Objectives of This Book   *3*
    Relationship of This Book to Earlier Treatments of
        Hypothesis-Testing Research in Anthropology   *4*
    Level of This Book   *5*

2. DESIGN OF HYPOTHESIS-TESTING RESEARCH IN ANTHROPOLOGY   *6*
    An Extended Hypothetical Example   *7*
    Some Research Paradigms   *9*
    Further Aspects of Research Design   *18*

3. RESEARCH DESIGN: SOME ANTHROPOLOGICAL EXAMPLES   *31*
    The Static Group Comparison in Anthropological Research   *31*
    The Pretest-Posttest Paradigm   *61*
    The Nonequivalent-Control-Group Paradigm   *65*
    Control-Group Paradigm   *70*
    Summary   *79*

4. THE PRAGMATICS OF HYPOTHESIS-TESTING RESEARCH IN
        ANTHROPOLOGY   *82*
        Site Selection   *82*
        Sample Selection   *84*
        Devising Measures   *87*
        Timing and the Fieldwork Process   *92*

5. SUMMARY AND SOME GENERAL IMPLICATIONS   *99*
        Explanation in Anthropology   *99*
        Research Design   *99*
        Research Pragmatics   *102*
        Implications   *104*

References   *112*

Recommended Readings   *117*

1 / Introduction

Anthropology, like other sciences, is concerned basically with two kinds of activity—description and explanation. In early anthropology description predominated. Many classic works of anthropology are largely or entirely descriptions of cultural forms. In recent years, however, there has been a shift of emphasis. While still concerned with producing accurate descriptions, most modern anthropologists attempt to go beyond description and provide explanations of cultural events— that is to say, they attempt to discover lawful regularities governing these events. As Anthony Wallace has recently commented (1970:3–4):

> Anthropologists have only lately begun to realize that new ethnographic description, like daily weather reporting, is an endless task. . . . Thus the problem for the theoretical anthropologist has shifted from the Linnaean classification of cultures and their aspects on a temporal or geographic continuum to the discovery and analysis of the laws of cultural process.

An essential step in the explanatory process is the development of hypotheses— tentative statements of the conditions that produce particular phenomena. Merely formulating hypotheses, of course, does little to advance our ability to explain. Many apparently sound hypotheses turn out, upon careful inquiry, to be invalid and therefore useless. If science did not possess some method of winnowing the chaff from the wheat, of weeding out erroneous hypotheses, little progress toward explanation would be possible. The process of testing hypotheses for validity, of verifying the fact that a relationship between factors does exist as hypothesized, is a central concern of research, for it is hypotheses that have survived *well-designed* tests that constitute the building blocks of explanation. This book deals with the conduct of hypothesis-testing research in anthropology. It presents the elements of research design within an anthropological framework and deals as well with certain pragmatic issues that, while they fall outside the realm of research design per se, have major implications for the execution of hypothesis-testing research.

Although there has been a shift in recent years toward an emphasis in anthropology on explanation and hypothesis-testing research, it should not be assumed that all contemporary anthropological inquiry deals explicitly with the testing of hypotheses. There is still substantial interest in exploratory descriptive studies. The fact that this book does not deal with the conduct of such studies should not be read as an indictment of exploratory description. Indeed, we explicitly acknowledge the value of descriptive studies, particularly when they are focused on types of sociocultural phenomena that are as yet virtually "uncharted" by anthropologists.

1

Broad descriptive studies are an important link in the chain of anthropological research, as they lay a foundation for subsequent more highly focused hypothesis-testing studies. Similarly, the principles of research design discussed in this book lead not to a wholesale rejection of traditional anthropological field methods but provide, rather, a vital supplement to them.

We expect, however, that emphasis in anthropology will continue to shift toward explanation and hypothesis-testing research. There seems to be growing acceptance of the view that "pure" unstructured description is not likely to uncover significant regularities in human behavior. As Harris has commented:

> The trouble is that a random sampling of any field of observation will prove beyond the shadow of doubt that nature is chaotic. One has merely to observe birds flying, smoke rising, clouds drifting, feathers floating, stones plummeting to realize that Galileo's formulation of the laws of motion could not possibly have resulted from the mere collection of facts. If one set out to note all the facts about a single grain of sand, all of the computers in the world could not store the information which could eventually be collected on that subject (1968:287–288).

The need to coordinate description with hypothesis testing, if we are to advance in the development of general anthropological laws, has been succinctly stated by E. E. Evans-Pritchard, who, in the course of a critique of the comparative method, concludes that "little advance can be made unless each new piece of research is done in relation to hypotheses, to confirm, reject or modify them" and who suggests, moreover, that the intensive field study "can only yield abundantly if each investigator is aware of and is prepared to test hypotheses put forward by others and does not in his own contribution just ignore them . . ." (1963:24).[1]

THEORIES AND THE ORIGIN OF HYPOTHESES

Given that hypotheses are the essential raw material for the development of explanations, what, one might well ask, is the origin of hypotheses? A partial answer is "theory." A theory is conventionally defined as a set of logically related principles that generate statements specifying the nature of the relationships between phenomena (variables). In the case of anthropology, the theories pertain to human behavior. Often one hears of "grand theory" or "middle-range theory" as though these were readily identifiable types of theory. .But for most social scientists, the level of theory is less vital than the fit between theory and reality. Examples of theories in anthropology include evolutionary theory, exchange theory, learning theory, coalition theory, location theory, and conflict theory, to name but a few.

We are interested in theories for many reasons, although two of them are particularly salient here. First, theories, by their very nature, permit us to summarize in terms of relatively few principles the nature of the relationships between a great many phenomena. It is more convenient, and hence, more valuable in some ultimate evolutionary sense, for humans to have and use such encompassing systems of thought. They simplify the task of dealing with reality. For the scientist, a theory

[1] We may note at this point, in fairness, that not all anthropologists are enthusiastic about the growth of hypothesis-testing research in anthropology. In our opinion, much of this opposition may be the result of confusing the character of the endeavor with its caricature. We will attempt to justify this opinion in our concluding remarks in Chapter 5.

will endure (be accepted or "believed") so long as the statements it generates provide the most adequate available way of dealing with (or responding to, depending upon your viewpoint) reality. And it is this feature of science (the comparative assessment of statements generated by different theories) that leads us directly to the second reason for our interest in theories: theories generate hypotheses that must be assessed.

Theories themselves cannot be "proved." The only thing that can happen to a theory, so far as scientists are concerned (at least "in theory"), is that it can be evaluated in terms of the extent to which the statements it generates about the nature of relationships between phenomena are accurate (that is, consistent with careful assessments against reality). This is a comparative process involving relative assessments of theories. To put it more simply, some theories don't "work" as well as others, and we can best evaluate different theories in these terms by systematically examining the various statements of relationship generated by them. These statements of relationship have a variety of names, but in general they are termed *hypotheses*. Theories generate many hypotheses, but until these hypotheses are rigorously assessed against reality, their validity (and hence their relative value) must remain in doubt. Hence a major goal of science (if we assume an even more basic goal is theory building) is assessing the relative value of hypotheses by testing them rigorously.

So far, this discussion of the relationship between theories and hypotheses makes it appear that scientists constantly dream up (and the choice of words is intentional) theories and then test the hypotheses generated by them. And indeed, many scientists do just that. On the other hand, many scientists first examine reality by testing hypotheses not associated with any particular theory, leaving theory building to a later phase of the research. Whether one works from "theory downward to reality" or from "reality upward to theory" (in other words, whether one takes a deductive or an inductive approach) one is doing science. Philosophers of science have, for centuries, debated the relative merits of these two strategies, and out of all this debate has come widespread recognition of the great value of both, and indeed, of the difficulty in distinguishing the two in many contexts.

ORGANIZATION AND OBJECTIVES OF THIS BOOK

In light of the above, this book is intended as a *guide for those who would undertake hypothesis-testing research* in sociocultural anthropology. As such, it is oriented primarily to the "how to do it" issues that of necessity would have to be considered in such a guide. But there is a second objective. It is also intended as a *guide for those who desire to evaluate the hypothesis-testing research of others*. The literature in anthropology is growing rapidly and an ever-increasing portion of it concerns hypothesis-testing research. Much of this is difficult and complex research, and it is necessary, therefore, to have guidelines for evaluation. Not surprisingly, the same principles that ought to guide the formulation and execution of such research can (and should) be used to evaluate it once it is completed.

The book is divided into three major sections, corresponding to Chapters 2, 3, and 4. In Chapter 2, basic principles of research design are developed. Chapter 3 illustrates these principles, using examples of hypothesis-testing research drawn from the anthropological literature and that of related disciplines. In Chapter 4 we discuss some important pragmatic factors that can influence the conduct of field research in sociocultural anthropology oriented (at least in part) to testing hypotheses. There is also a brief concluding chapter, Chapter 5, which provides an overview of the issues we have raised and includes some general comments regarding the implications of these issues for contemporary anthropology.

It should be pointed out that both authors of this book are sociocultural anthropologists and that we have had in mind colleagues with similar interests when we wrote this book. Thus, our research examples in Chapters 2 and 3 are drawn from sociocultural anthropology and our discussion in Chapter 4 of pragmatics in the execution of hypothesis-testing research assumes the researcher is a sociocultural anthropologist. We would emphasize, however, that the basic principles of hypothesis testing apply to all subfields of anthropology; indeed, they are common to all sciences. To be sure, we expect there will be variability in the implementation of these principles from one subfield to another. These differences can be attributed in general to the nature of the hypotheses being tested, and, in particular, to the nature of the variables in these hypotheses. Additional chapters would have to be written by others qualified to do so in order to indicate what the practical issues would be for the archaeologist or physical anthropologist who might wish to apply these principles in his field situation. We would expect many of these issues to be the same, and to the extent that they are, this book is relevant to non-sociocultural anthropologists. It has not been our intention, however, to consider all these other pragmatic issues.[2]

RELATIONSHIP OF THIS BOOK TO EARLIER TREATMENTS OF HYPOTHESIS-TESTING RESEARCH IN ANTHROPOLOGY

From a very early date, anthropologists have been concerned with the rigor of their hypothesis-testing research. Boas, Kroeber, Malinowski, Radcliffe-Brown, and many other anthropological luminaries in the early part of this century come to mind in this regard, even though the greater part of their work was oriented to description. In her recent autobiography (*Blackberry Winter*), Margaret Mead stresses her interest in methodology, noting that she had a solid preparation in psychology in the "use of samples, tests, and systematic inventories of behavior" (1972:139). Moreover, she indicates that her fieldwork in Samoa (which we discuss at length in Chapter 3) was not concerned so much with describing the culture as a whole but rather was focused on a specific problem.[3] Other considera-

---

[2] And in this context, we may also note that we will use the term "anthropologist" throughout this book in a *general* sense. This usage is conventional and, in this book at least, is intentional. We have a general anthropological audience in mind, along with our admitted emphasis on sociocultural anthropology.

[3] In this same part of her autobiography, Mead (1972:142) decries the tradition so prominent in anthropology in the United States (in her day as well as ours) of giving minimal attention to the "how's" of anthropological research. For her, such a system is "wasteful" if it assumes that if "young fieldworkers do not give up in despair, go mad, ruin their health, or die, they do, after a fashion, become anthropologists." We could hardly agree more, and would contend that the principles discussed in this book should be included among the "how's" with which anthropologists should be familiar.

tions of method go back to the very earliest efforts in anthropology, including, most classically perhaps, Tylor's consideration (1889) of various "adhesions" (correlations) in marriage customs around the world. But probably the best known of previous efforts to introduce more elaborately structured research designs into anthropological fieldwork is the "method of controlled comparisons" (see Eggan 1954, for an extended discussion of this popular method).[4]

Such pioneering efforts in anthropology have been followed over the years by scores of "designed" hypothesis-testing sociocultural field-research efforts. The resulting monographs often include prefaces and appendices discussing the methods used. Although the principles we discuss in this book are often not made very explicit in these discussions, they can be detected (and indeed, we would recommend that students examine these statements in order to become more familiar both with the traditions of anthropological research design and with the principles we discuss in this book). In any case, there is ample precedent for the present discussion of research design in anthropology, and we acknowledge with due appreciation the work of our predecessors. Our objective in this book has been to build on the foundations they have laid.

LEVEL OF THIS BOOK

We would also stress, finally, that this book is a general and introductory treatment of the principles of anthropological research design. Problems of measurement, considerations of chance, sample selection, and paradigm development are treated in greater detail and at a more advanced level in the sociological, psychological, and, to a lesser extent, in the anthropological literature on research methods. We do not discuss, for example, the complex time-series or factorial paradigms (often termed "designs" in other sources). These omissions are intentional. We believe beginning students in anthropology should be familiar with the principles of research design, but we also believe initial exposure to the full complexity of these issues will go beyond the needs of most anthropology students in introductory courses. Our objective is to stimulate an interest in the subject of research design, as a stimulus both to designing better research and to evaluating existing research. We hope the discussion of the basic principles of research design will motivate the reader to pursue more advanced treatments elsewhere.[5] We would add, lest the reader assume otherwise, that the difficulties a researcher in anthropology will face in attempting to utilize these more sophisticated methods will provide ample opportunity for creative, productive, and rewarding work.

[4] This method, which has received widespread praise in anthropology, is (as we point out in Chapter 3), essentially a variety of what we term the "static group comparison" paradigm—a paradigm whose basic characteristics are discussed in Chapter 2.

[5] Some of the more informative of these advanced discussions of research design for the social sciences may be found in Blalock (1964), Campbell and Stanley (1969), Cochran and Cox (1957), Edwards (1960), Kirk (1968), Lindquist (1953) and Miller (1964).

2 / Design of hypothesis-testing research in anthropology

An essential part of the explanatory process in all sciences, as we noted in Chapter 1, is the formulation of hypotheses, or statements that attempt to specify the conditions producing particular phenomena. Thus, when an anthropologist sets out to explain some cultural phenomenon—let us say, for example, the nuclear family form of household organization—he or she begins by formulating hypotheses about the conditions that give rise to it. The hypotheses, as we noted in Chapter 1, usually derive directly or indirectly from some set of general assumptions or general theory about human behavior. Such a hypothesis might take the following form: "As a culture becomes industrialized, the proportion of nuclear family households will increase." The formulation of such a hypothesis is only an initial stage in the explanatory process, however. A second and crucial step is *testing* the hypothesis. It is only by attempting to establish the truth or falsity of such hypotheses that we gain the knowledge we need to construct explanations of the cultural phenomena with which we deal. It is the business of testing hypotheses—which sounds deceptively simple, but in practice often proves extremely difficult—that constitutes research design, the topic of this book.

It will be useful to begin our discussion of research design by examining in more detail the nature of a hypothesis. *A hypothesis is a tentative statement of what condition(s) will produce the phenomenon of interest.* It will be clear from this definition that *a hypothesis involves a statement of relationship.* Every hypothesis must specify a relationship between *at least two variables.* One of these variables represents *the phenomenon the researcher is trying to account for.* This is the *dependent variable.* The other variable represents *the factor that is thought to produce changes in the dependent variable.* This is the *independent variable.* A hypothesis must also specify the *nature of the relationship* between the independent and dependent variables.

Thus, in our specimen hypothesis—as a culture becomes industrialized, the proportion of nuclear family households will increase—industrialization is the independent variable that is held to produce a change in the dependent variable, the proportion of nuclear family households. The nature of the relationship is that as the independent variable increases, the dependent variable also increases. We can diagram the hypothesis in this manner:

INDEPENDENT VARIABLE	NATURE OF RELATIONSHIP	DEPENDENT VARIABLE
Industrialization	increases	the proportion of nuclear family households.

Not all hypotheses are this simple, of course. Some show a considerably more complex structure. The type of hypothesis represented by our example is, however, very commonly encountered. In order to increase your familiarity with this type of hypothesis, let us consider three more hypotheses that deal with different subject matters but share this same basic structure:

1. The greater the importance of agriculture in the subsistence economy of a culture, the more its child-training practices will stress "obedience."
2. Private ownership of land will be uncommon in cultures where the subsistence economy emphasizes hunting and gathering.
3. Sorcery will be more frequent in cultures with weak judicial institutions.

When these three hypotheses are diagrammed, their structural similarity is readily apparent. Each contains an independent and a dependent variable and a phrase specifying the nature of the relationship between them.

INDEPENDENT VARIABLE	NATURE OF RELATIONSHIP	DEPENDENT VARIABLE
1. Importance of agriculture in the subsistence economy	increases	stress on "compliance" in child training.
2. Importance of hunting and gathering in the subsistence economy	decreases	private land ownership.
3. Weakness of judicial institutions	increases	frequency of sorcery.

We are now ready to address the problem of how an anthropologist goes about testing a hypothesis. Put most simply, *testing a hypothesis involves exposing it to a situation that can show it to be false.* If the hypothesis survives a *well-designed* attempt at falsifying it, the researcher is justified in having increased confidence in its validity, although, very often, he will wish to subject it to still further tests before concluding that it is correct (and even then the conclusion remains tentative).

AN EXTENDED HYPOTHETICAL EXAMPLE

In order that we may explore some approaches to hypothesis testing, we are going to ask you to imagine a hypothetical research situation. Let us suppose an anthropologist is studying a peasant society undergoing rapid modernization. Many casual observers have reported that peasant villages in the more developed areas of this society seem to have experienced a decrease in cohesion—that is to say, a decrease in the degree to which people living within them are friendly and "neighborly" toward one another. The anthropologist becomes interested in explaining this apparent decrease in village cohesion. The reason for his interest in the phenomenon of village cohesion might be that he believes the mental health of villagers will be adversely affected by a decrease in the amount of friendliness and neighborliness in their village. Whatever the reason for his interest, if he is to account for decreases in village cohesion, he must attempt to develop and test a hypothesis in which village cohesion is the dependent variable.

Typically, in developing hypotheses, an anthropologist will draw on many kinds of information. Our anthropologist, for example, will no doubt draw upon his general knowledge of human behavior. Also, his anthropological training has equipped him with knowledge of many very general hypotheses about cultural and psychological phenomena. He may be able to relate some of these hypotheses to his research situation as an aid in developing a specific hypothesis about decreases in village cohesion in this society. One potentially relevant general hypothesis which might occur to him is the proposition that the more the members of a group depend upon one another, the greater will be the group's cohesion. The anthropologist feels that villages in this area may legitimately be considered to constitute a type of group. He knows also, from the ethnographic information available to him, that the residents of these villages have traditionally been dependent on one another in many ways. This leads him to wonder whether he might develop a hypothesis that relates decreases in village cohesion to some sort of decrease in the mutual dependence of the villagers.

One of the most important ways, he knows, in which members of a village have been mutually dependent is in connection with irrigation. Villagers have traditionally relied on a highly complex system of irrigation works to provide water for their crops. These irrigation works require constant maintenance. The labor involved in keeping the various dikes, dams, and primary channels in good repair is quite considerable and is far beyond the capabilities of a single individual or family. Traditionally, the members of a village have worked together as a team to perform regular maintenance on the portions of the irrigation system upon which they rely.

From his field observations, the anthropologist is aware that, as part of the modernization process, a technological innovation which has a major impact on the system of irrigation maintenance is gradually being introduced into the region. This innovation is the windmill. The region is fortunate in having strong and nearly constant prevailing winds that make it ideally suited for the use of these wind-powered pumps. There is, moreover, a high water table that can easily be tapped by shallow, hand-dug wells. As a result, by acquiring several windmills and digging shallow wells in his fields, a farmer can make himself independent of the old irrigation system. In so doing he frees himself of the heavy labor involved in irrigation system maintenance and obtains a more reliable source of water. (The mountain springs that supply the irrigation system are undependable and sometimes go dry at critical times.) There is, not surprisingly, a strong demand on the part of the farmers for the windmills. They are, however, still in short supply.

These windmills are being provided to the villagers under a very generous time-payment plan by the government agricultural development agency. Since the supply of windmills is limited, it is not possible to provide them simultaneously to all farmers. The agency fears that if windmills are made available to some farmers in a village but not to others, those who have been left out will feel they have been treated unfairly. To avoid this, it has been decided to provide windmills, as they become available, on a village-by-village basis; if a village is designated to receive windmills, *all* farmers in that village will receive them.

When the members of a village have received windmills, they can and do allow the old irrigation system to fall into disrepair. When this happens, they become much less dependent on one another, since collective activity to maintain irrigation works is no longer necessary. This, it seems to the anthropologist, could very well be a key factor underlying decreases in village cohesion.

Having reached this point in his analysis of the situation, the anthropologist is now prepared to formulate a specific hypothesis to account for decreased village cohesion. This hypothesis takes the following form: "Villages which receive windmills and whose members therefore experience reduced mutual dependence will decrease in cohesion." Diagramming the hypothesis in our usual fashion, we obtain the following:

INDEPENDENT VARIABLE	NATURE OF RELATIONSHIP	DEPENDENT VARIABLE
Use of windmills	decreases	village cohesion.

Before this hypothesis can be tested, a way must be found to measure the dependent variable. Without going into detail regarding the procedures which can be employed in the development of a measure for such a variable (some of these techniques will be discussed in Chapter 4), let us assume that the anthropologist is able to develop a satisfactory measure of cohesion. This measure, let us say, involves the use of a standardized interview. The interview consists of a number of questions concerning the degree of friendliness between neighbors—for example, "Do your neighbors usually greet you in a cordial manner when they see you for the first time in the morning?" For each question to which the informant answers "Yes," one point is scored. To measure cohesion in a village the anthropologist administers the interview to the adult members of the village. Their scores are then averaged to produce a cohesion score for the village as a whole.

SOME RESEARCH PARADIGMS[1]

The Pretest–Posttest Paradigm

Having developed a measure of cohesion, there are a number of basic approaches the anthropologist might utilize to test his hypothesis. One strategy he might adopt

[1] The term "paradigm" is used here in its basic dictionary sense of "pattern" or "model." It is simply a way of giving emphasis to the models used in research design. Paradigm will be defined and discussed in this sense in some detail throughout this chapter and in the remainder of the book.

is to focus on a group of villages that are about to receive windmills. *Before* the windmills are made available, he administers his interview in each village. *After* the pumps have been in use for some time, he returns and administers the interview a second time. In this way he determines whether the introduction of windmills to their villages has generally been followed by a decrease in village cohesion as is predicted by the hypothesis.

It will be useful to have a simple notational system we can use to diagram an approach such as this. Such a notational scheme will greatly facilitate comparisons among various approaches to hypothesis testing which will be discussed. The system we will employ for this purpose is that of Campbell and Stanley (1966). In this system an "X" represents exposure to a high level of the independent variable and an "O" (for "observation") represents a measurement of the dependent variable. We can diagram the research situation just described as follows:

$$O \qquad X \qquad O$$

This should be read, from left to right, as indicating that measurements of the dependent variable (symbolized by the first O) were taken from the group of villages under study. These villages were exposed to a high level of the independent variable (windmills were given to the villages) as symbolized by the X. Then a second wave of measurements was taken (symbolized by the second O).

Any pattern of measurements and exposure to a high level of an independent variable such as is represented by this diagram can be referred to as a *research paradigm*.[2] You will encounter several different research paradigms in anthropological research. This particular one is known as the *pretest–posttest paradigm*.[3]

Use of the pretest-posttest paradigm, then, is one approach to the testing of a hypothesis. Let us now ask the question: "How *adequate* a test of the hypothesis does this paradigm provide?" It may appear that the pretest–posttest paradigm constitutes a rather conclusive test of the hypothesis. However, upon careful consideration, this paradigm proves to be subject to certain types of error that may lead the researcher to a mistaken conclusion about the validity of his hypothesis. For example, one source of error that poses a threat to (and hence weakens) this paradigm has to do with the effects of *extraneous variables*. These are *variables other than the independent variable that might affect the dependent variable.*

To illustrate the kind of mistaken inferences which can result from the effects of extraneous variables (in this paradigm, at least), let us assume that a sharp

---

[2] As the second part of this chapter will show, there is more to research than "choosing" a research paradigm. However, the research paradigm is perhaps the single most crucial element in a research design. Although the paradigms with which we will deal do not exhaust the possible paradigms that may usefully be employed in research, most anthropologists have used a basic or modified version of one of the four we will discuss. Thus, a sound understanding of the characteristics of these basic paradigms is invaluable for evaluating the research of others and designing research of one's own. It is for these reasons that we have chosen to begin this work with a discussion of research paradigms.

[3] In the interest of fostering a standardized terminology for research paradigms, we have chosen to adopt the terminology used by Campbell and Stanley in *Experimental and Quasi-Experimental Designs for Research* (1966) to designate the paradigms discussed in this book.

decrease in cohesion *is* found to have occurred in the windmill-receiving villages. While this result is consistent with the hypothesis, there unfortunately is no assurance that the decrease is due to the independent variable, the introduction of windmills. It could instead be due to some extraneous variable(s) to which the villages were exposed during the time the independent variable was introduced.

It might have been, for example, that in the interval between the first and second measurements, a great many newcomers moved into the villages owing to political turmoil in a neighboring district. The presence of these relative strangers might in itself be expected to decrease village cohesion. Alternately, perhaps some incident has occurred that has created animosity between two major religious groups in the area. Assuming most villages have members from both sects, such an incident could set villager against villager and account for the lowered level of cohesion. Changes in extraneous variables such as these can thus give rise to an erroneous inference that the independent variable caused a change in the dependent variable, when in fact it had no effect.

The problem of extraneous factors is not limited to situations in which the dependent variable changes as predicted. An extraneous factor may also act to cancel out changes in the dependent variable that would otherwise have occurred. Let us suppose that in actuality the introduction of windmills did have the effect of decreasing village cohesion. If shortly afterwards something else happened to increase village cohesion—such as an outbreak of banditry, which, because of the need for cooperative defense, made the villagers even more dependent upon one another than in the past—the drop in cohesion stemming from the use of the windmills might easily be concealed by the rise in cohesion owing to the banditry. In such a situation, the researcher might erroneously infer that the independent variable had no effect when in fact it did.

Another source of error to which the pretest–posttest paradigm is subject has to do with possible *reactive effects of the measurement procedure* employed. It is possible for a measurement procedure itself to react upon—that is, to cause a change in—the dependent variable. In the present example, it is conceivable that the structured interview which inquires about the amount of "neighborliness" in a village might have the effect of reminding villagers of incidents in which neighbors had failed to be "neighborly." The temporary resentment thus created might cause them to be less friendly toward one another for a time. Thus, cohesion could be temporarily decreased due to the reactive effects of the measurement process alone. If this temporary decrease in cohesion were detected by the second wave of measurements an investigator might erroneously infer that the independent variable was responsible for the change.

This discussion of the pretest–posttest paradigm illustrates a crucial point. *The validity of a hypothesis cannot be established simply by obtaining research results that are consistent with it. Plausible rival hypotheses must also be ruled out.* The reason a pretest–posttest paradigm does not provide a very powerful test of a hypothesis is that, as we have seen, two plausible rival hypotheses cannot be rejected: that a change in the dependent variable might be due to the effects of extraneous variables, or that it might be due to reactive measurement effects. Either or both of these rival hypotheses, since they cannot be rejected, may be suspected of having masked the true effect of the introduction of windmills.

The Static-Group-Comparison Paradigm

Let us now consider another approach the anthropologist might employ in attempting to test his hypothesis. Instead of observing the same group of villages before and after windmills are allocated to them, as in the preceding example, the anthropologist might elect to compare the level of cohesion in a group of villages which have already received windmills with that in a group of villages without them.

In order to diagram the research paradigm represented by this approach it will be necessary to introduce another convention into our notational system. We will use the same symbols as before, but will represent each group by a separate row of symbols. We can now diagram this paradigm, which has been designated the *static group comparison*, as follows:

Treatment Group	X	O

Comparison Group		O

This can be read as indicating that the treatment group, represented by the upper row of symbols, was exposed to a high level of the independent variable—that is, was allocated windmills—and then received measurements. The lower row of symbols shows that the comparison group received measurement only. In discussing paradigms such as this in which more than one group is used it will be useful to have a simple way of distinguishing between the groups. We will therefore use the term *treatment group* to refer to a group, such as the first one here, that is exposed to a high level of the independent variable—in other words, whose row of symbols contains an "X." The term *comparison group*[4] will be used to designate a group that receives measurements but is not exposed to a high level of the independent variable—in other words, to any group whose line of symbols does not contain an "X," such as the second group in this example.[5]

Now let us explore the adequacy of the static group comparison as a means of testing a hypothesis. Suppose that, after conducting a static group comparison of villages with windmills and of those without them, our anthropologist finds that the group of villages with windmills does indeed score lower on the dependent variable of cohesion. How strongly does this result support the hypothesis? An

---

[4] We use the term "comparison group" in preference to the commonly used term "control group" since this latter term is more precisely limited to a group that is known, or can be assumed, to be equivalent to the treatment group prior to the introduction of the independent variable.

[5] We have indicated that an X in the treatment group row of symbols indicates a high level of exposure to the independent variable. It is this exposure to a *high* level of the independent variable that distinguishes the treatment group from the comparison group. Consequently, this means that from time to time a comparison group *may* be exposed to the independent variable, although in order to be a true comparison group this exposure must be *lower* than the exposure received by the treatment group. In anthropological research, as in the other social sciences, comparison groups frequently are exposed to low levels of the independent variable. Thus, the absence of an X in the comparison group row of symbols does not necessarily indicate that the comparison group receives no exposure to the independent variable, but only that it is not exposed to a high level of the variable, as in the treatment group.

initial assessment may be made by comparing this paradigm to the previous one discussed—the pretest–posttest paradigm.

A major advantage of the static-group-comparison over the pretest–posttest paradigm is that it is possible, using the former, to reduce the likelihood of errors due to extraneous variables. *If the treatment and control groups are affected in the same manner by extraneous variables, a difference in the two groups' scores on the dependent variable cannot be ascribed to extraneous factors since these factors are "controlled"—are the same for both groups.* It must be emphasized that the effects of extraneous variables are controlled *only* to the extent that both groups experience the same extraneous factors to the same degree. If one group is less subject to extraneous factors, control over this source of error is weakened or lost entirely.

Let us suppose our anthropologist is able to make a strong case that his treatment and comparison groups are, by and large, exposed to extraneous factors of the same degree and kind. If he can do this, there is relatively little chance that a difference in cohesion between the two groups is due to the effects of extraneous variables.

Again, in contrast to the pretest–posttest paradigm, the static group comparison is not subject to reactive effects of measurements. Reaction effects occur, as you will recall, when the measurement process itself produces a change in the dependent variable. There is only one way the effect of measurement reaction can be confounded with the effect of the independent variable. This is when there is a measurement of the dependent variable prior to or at the same time as the operation of the independent variable. Since both groups in the static group comparison receive only postmeasurements (that is, after the independent variable has operated), it can safely be assumed that changes (if any) in the dependent variable are not due to measurement reaction effects. Thus, the static group comparison is free from the second source of error that plagues the pretest–posttest paradigm.

The static group comparison is, then, superior to the pretest–posttest paradigm in that it is not susceptible to reactive effects of measurement procedures and it offers some defense against the effects of extraneous variables. However, these advantages are to some extent counterbalanced by its susceptibility to a third source of error that does *not* affect the pretest–posttest paradigm.

The static group comparison is highly vulnerable to errors arising from "selection." *Selection* may be said to have occurred *whenever a treatment group differs from its comparison group because of the way in which the cases for the two groups were selected.*[6] Selection may cause treatment and comparison groups to differ in a number of ways. From the standpoint of assessing the effect of the independent variable, the most serious effect of selection is when it causes a treatment group to have a different score on the dependent variable from that of the comparison group. Such a difference resulting from selection alone may easily be

---

[6] The use of the term "selection" for this source of error should not be taken as implying that the agent who does the selecting is necessarily the investigator himself or is always human. In the case of many independent variables studied by anthropologists, the selection of cases to receive exposure to the independent variable is out of the hands of the researcher himself and is decided by persons over whom he has no control, or by "nature" (for example, it is "nature" that "decides" which villages receive abundant rainfall and which do not).

mistaken for the effect of the independent variable, posing the danger that the researcher will conclude that the independent variable has had an effect when in fact it may have had none.

To illustrate this problem, let us return to the research example at hand. If the anthropologist carries out a static group comparison by measuring cohesion in a group of villages which have already received windmills and in a group still lacking them, he has no assurance that the villages which received windmills were not lower in cohesion than the others to begin with owing to the manner in which they were selected. It might have been the case, for example, that because of domestic political considerations, larger villages were given priority in the allocation of windmills. If we assume that village cohesion might be influenced in some degree by size, large villages generally being less cohesive than small ones, we might reasonably expect the group of villages which received the windmills to have been lower in cohesion to start with. Even if the introduction of windmills had no effect, the treatment-group villages would score lower on cohesion due to the effect of selection. Thus, with the static group comparison there is a very real danger of the researcher mistaking the effect of selection for the effect of the independent variable.

The Nonequivalent-Control-Group Paradigm

Let us examine still another approach the anthropologist might employ in assessing the validity of his hypothesis. This time, as in the case of the pretest–posttest paradigm, he elects to focus on a group of villages that are about to receive windmills and to obtain measures of cohesion from the villages before and after the windmills have been introduced. He does not stop here, however. On the two occasions when he obtains measurements of cohesion from this group of villages, he also undertakes the measurement of cohesion in a second group of villages that does not receive windmills.

The paradigm representing this research situation is termed the *nonequivalent-control-group paradigm* and may be diagrammed as follows:

Treatment Group	O	X	O
Comparison Group	O		O

Reading from left to right, as with the previous diagrams, the first pair of "O's" indicates that both the treatment and comparison groups received a measurement of the dependent variable before the treatment group was exposed to a high level of the independent variable ("X"). Then both groups received a second measurement of the dependent variable.

After the data collection is complete, the researcher computes a "gain score" for each case[7] by subtracting its score on the premeasurement from the score it received on the postmeasurement. (It should be noted that a so-called "gain score" may in

---

[7] The term "case" is used throughout this book as a general designation for the units of interest to the investigator, whether these cases be villages, persons, cultures, or whatever.

fact be negative if a case has a postmeasurement score smaller than its premeasurement score.) He then compares the gain scores of the treatment and comparison groups to see if the results are as predicted by the hypothesis. In our example, if the introduction of the windmills has the hypothesized effect of reducing cohesion scores, this should cause the average gain score for the treatment group to be significantly more negative than that of the comparison group.[8]

The nonequivalent-control-group paradigm has substantial advantages over the two other paradigms we have considered. It is clearly superior to the pretest–posttest paradigm in that error due to reactive effects of the measurement procedure is controlled. Even if the first measurements react upon—cause a change in—the dependent variable, this will be true for *both* groups. Thus, reactive effects of measurement procedures alone cannot contribute to a difference in the two groups' gain scores.

This paradigm is also clearly superior to the static-group-comparison paradigm in that it controls for the effect of selection. Because it is the gain scores of the two groups that are being compared, rather than single raw scores for each group, differences due to selection cannot be mistaken for the effects of the independent variable.

As with the static group comparison, the nonequivalent-control-group paradigm offers some defense against error due to extraneous variables. Again, to the extent that the treatment and comparison groups are affected in the *same* manner by extraneous variables, these extraneous factors cannot contribute to a difference in gain scores between the two groups, and their effects cannot therefore masquerade as the effect of the independent variable.

A source of error to which the nonequivalent-control-group paradigm (together with the static group comparison) is vulnerable is error due to *interaction effects involving selection*. Although selection per se will not give rise to erroneous inferences when the nonequivalent-control-group paradigm is used, as was explained above, the effects of selection may interact with other factors to produce misleading results. One commonly encountered problem is interaction between selection and extraneous factors. That is, it often happens that differences between treatment and comparison groups due to selection cause the two groups to be differentially affected by extraneous variables.

An example of this interaction effect, in the context of our anthropologist's research, would occur if windmills were only given to villages near a road (perhaps because of ease of transport). If all the remaining villages were located away from a road, this would create a situation in which the treatment group was made up of villages enjoying better communications than those in the comparison group. This difference between the two groups due to selection (that is, to being near or far from a road) could interact with extraneous factors and result in the two groups having different gain scores even if the independent variable had had no effect. Thus, the fact that the treatment group is made up of villages close to a road could mean that these windmill-receiving villages will also subsequently

---

[8] That is, the cohesion scores for the villages in the treatment group would be expected to decrease more between the first and second measurements than would the scores for the comparison-group villages.

receive better opportunities for city employment, better educational opportunities, and more effective police protection. These extraneous factors may all conceivably act to lower village cohesion. Thus, their effects on the treatment group may be mistaken for that of the independent variable.

The Control-Group Paradigm

A research paradigm that contributes a great deal to preventing errors due to interaction effects involving selection is the *control-group paradigm.* This paradigm closely resembles the nonequivalent-control-group paradigm except for one important aspect. In this paradigm the cases (such as villages) are *randomly assigned to the treatment and comparison groups*, thereby maximizing the likelihood that the two groups will be equivalent (that there will be no substantial differences between them attributable to selection). The control-group paradigm is diagrammed as follows:

Treatment Group	R	O	X	O
Comparison Group	R	O		O

This diagram is nearly identical to that of the nonequivalent-control-group paradigm. The difference is the addition of the symbol "R," which indicates that the cases were randomly assigned to both the treatment and control groups.

To apply the control-group paradigm, the anthropologist must obviously be in a position to assign villages (or other cases) to treatment and control groups. He must, moreover, assign villages to these two groups on some *random* basis so that each village has an *equal chance of being included* in the treatment group. Let us suppose the anthropologist in our example has sufficient influence in the agricultural development agency to be allowed to designate the villages that will receive windmills. He may then elect to employ the control-group paradigm. To do this, he selects a sample of villages. He randomly assigns half of the villages to the treatment group and the other half to the comparison group.[9] The effect of randomly assigning villages to the treatment and comparison groups is that the possibility of there being substantial differences between the two groups due to selection is reduced to a minimum. If, for example, one group of villages within the sample is somehow distinct from the rest, let us say by virtue of being located near roads, it is unlikely these distinctive villages will be concentrated in either the treatment or comparison groups because the villages are assigned on a *random* basis. The most likely result is that these distinctive villages will be more or less evenly divided between the two groups. This randomization procedure thus

---

[9] He will probably find it convenient in making these assignments to utilize a table of random numbers. To use such a table, he must assign each village a number. If, for example, he is working with a sample of 40 villages, he may number the villages from 1 through 40. He then will search through the table of random numbers for these numbers, assigning the villages bearing the first 20 numbers he finds in the range 1 to 40 to the treatment group and those bearing the remaining numbers to the comparison group (or vice versa). Since the numbers in a table of random numbers are in random order, this ensures that a random assignment of villages to the two groups is made.

minimizes the possibility of major differences between the groups arising through selection. Consequently, the possibility of significant interaction effects involving selection is also minimized.

It should be emphasized, however, that use of the control-group paradigm with its random assignment of cases does not completely eliminate the possibility of selection effects or consequent interactions between selection and other factors. The researcher may have "bad luck" and the villages in the treatment group may still end up being distinctive from those of the comparison group, despite their random assignment. (Random *assignment* is fairly easy if it is possible at all. Drawing a random *sample* is very hard. This facet of research is discussed later.) However, the advantage of this design in minimizing the possibility of such effects should not be underestimated. The researcher is often in a position of near or complete ignorance concerning important differences between cases. Under these circumstances he can do no better than to trust to the control-group paradigm, with its attendant randomization, to hold to a minimum the possibility of selection effects or of interaction effects involving differences due to selection.[10]

The Four Paradigms, in Summary

Perhaps the most important general point which has emerged from this discussion of basic research paradigms is that verification of a hypothesis involves more than simply obtaining research results consistent with that hypothesis. One must also attempt to structure research in such a way that plausible *alternative interpretations* of the research results can be ruled out. It is important in this connection that the researcher be aware of alternative interpretations which emerge from the structure of the research process itself—that is, from the research paradigm. In commenting on the four research paradigms included in this book, we have noted four common error sources that can be the bases of alternative interpretations of research results. Since these generally lead to a mistaken inference that changes or differences in the dependent variable are due to the independent variable when in fact they may be due to a number of other factors or "effects," these are termed *rival hypotheses*. The factors that are the bases of the four major rival hypotheses are: (1) *the effects of selection*; (2) *reactive measurement effects*; (3) *the effects of uncontrolled extraneous variables*; and (4) *interaction effects involving selection*.

---

[10] It is important to note a frequently used variant of the control-group paradigm that differs from the standard version in omitting the premeasurements:

R	X	O
R		O

In this version, which we may call the *posttest-only control-group paradigm*, it is assumed that the randomization process will cause the treatment and comparison groups to be equivalent prior to the introduction of the independent variable, thus making it possible to dispense with the premeasurements. This is a defensible assumption, since, as we noted, randomization is generally quite effective in equating two groups. The standard version of the control-group paradigm has the advantage, however, of providing a definite indication of whether randomization has in fact equated the two groups on at least the dependent variable.

Table 2.1 provides a summary of the strengths and weaknesses of the four basic paradigms in regard to these rival hypotheses. As you will have gathered by now, the control-group paradigm is the strongest of the four. The nonequivalent-control-group paradigm occupies an intermediate position, and the static group comparison together with the pretest–posttest paradigm make up the bottom rank.

The conditions of the research situation obviously will dictate to a large degree which of the paradigms can be employed. Thus, the difficult research conditions under which an anthropologist must work may often make it necessary to settle for a relatively weak paradigm such as one or another variant of the static group comparison and to try to compensate for its weaknesses by special techniques (some of which will be discussed in Chapter 3). However, it should be clear by now that it is only good research strategy to apply the strongest possible paradigm which conditions permit. Thus, if the research situation were one in which the nonequivalent-control-group paradigm was feasible, it would be foolish for the investigator to settle for the significantly weaker static group comparison.

TABLE 2.1   SOURCES OF ERROR[a]

Type of paradigm	Selection	Reactive measurement effects	Effects of extraneous variables	Interaction effects involving selection
Pretest–posttest O X O		—	—	
Static–group comparison X O O	—	+	+[b]	—
Nonequivalent control-group O X O O . O	+	+	+[b]	—
Control-group R O X O R O O	+	+	+	+

[a] A minus indicates a weakness in regard to the source of error. A plus indicates that the paradigm is resistant to the source of error. A blank indicates that the source of error is not applicable to the paradigm.
[b] The static-group and nonequivalent-control-group paradigms are resistant to the effects of extraneous variables to the extent that these variables affect both groups in the same manner.

FURTHER ASPECTS OF RESEARCH DESIGN

There is much more to designing research than choosing the most powerful feasible research paradigm. Consequently, the remainder of this chapter will be directed to a discussion of other vital considerations in the design of hypothesis-testing research. Specifically, we will consider three aspects: measurement, replicability, and the role of chance.

First, regarding measurement, we have seen that it is necessary to somehow measure the dependent variable. Otherwise, one has no way of knowing if, or to what extent, this variable is behaving as the hypothesis predicts. Also, as will be shown in subsequent discussion, it is sometimes highly desirable to measure the independent variable. In any case, measurement is an indispensable part of research, and it is an inescapable fact that some measures are better than others. We will emphasize this in our discussion below. Second, regarding replicability, it is essential, in research of the type we are discussing here, to give a complete description of the procedures used in testing the hypothesis so others may evaluate the results in terms of the adequacy of these procedures, as well as consider attempting another test of the same hypothesis. Third, it is equally essential that the research consider the results in the light of what is essentially another rival hypothesis— chance. Only if chance is ruled out can the results be meaningfully assessed.

Measurement

The adequacy of a measure may be assessed in a number of ways.[11] We will consider the three most important criteria in assessing a measure; these are reliability, validity, and precision.

Reliability   The reliability of a measure refers to its stability or consistency— that is, to be *the extent to which it will give the same results when repeatedly applied to the same situation.* A method that can often be employed to assess the reliability of measures used in anthropological research is the *test–retest method.* To use this method the investigator looks for a situation in which he can be reasonably confident the variable being measured will remain constant. He then applies his measuring device at least twice to obtain an indication of how consistent it is. The first measurement constitutes the "test" and the second measurement (and succeeding measurements after that, if any) the "retest(s)."

To exemplify the test–retest method let us suppose a researcher wished to assess the reliability of a measure of temperature using the test–retest approach. To do this he will need a situation in which temperature can be expected to remain constant. He is able to meet this requirement, let us say, by finding a cave far below ground where he can be reasonably confident the temperature will remain at a constant level over long periods of time. He may then use his measure to ascertain the cave's temperature on a number of occasions—the first occasion being the test and subsequent occasions the retests. If the measure is a reliable one, such as a good thermometer, the results of the different trials will show a high degree of consistency—the mercury will reach very nearly the same point every time he takes the thermometer into the cave.

Reliability, of course, is a relative thing. Even the best measures will show some variation from trial to trial. If the researcher measured the temperature in the constant-temperature cave on five occasions he might find the thermometer readings looked like this:

64.9   65.2   65.0   64.8   65.1

---

[11] In anthropology, concern for the adequacy of measures is one of the least-developed facets of research design. Given the vital role of measurement in all sciences, this area of weakness would benefit greatly from extensive creative work by anthropologists. We will discuss measurement from a somewhat more pragmatic perspective in Chapter 4.

He could *not* say the thermometer was *perfectly* reliable. However, he could say it is highly reliable compared to some other possible measures. If he used a group of people to measure the temperature on five different occasions by estimation, he would probably find that their average estimates looked something like this:

60   75   58   71   63

This latter measure would obviously be rejected in favor of the far more reliable thermometer.

Let us now explore the use of the test–retest method in establishing the reliability of measures used in anthropological research. In discussing research paradigms, we envisioned a research situation in which an anthropologist was studying the effects of windmills on village cohesion. At that time we simply assumed he had been able to develop a satisfactory measure of cohesion. We did not indicate how the anthropologist might have gone about determining the adequacy of his measure. One course of action he might have taken to determine the measure's reliability is to make use of the test–retest method. He might do this by administering the standardized interview he is employing as his measure of cohesion in ten villages. After a period of time, he could return and administer the same interview in the same ten villages. *If* the anthropologist can safely assume the measurement is nonreactive and *if* he can safely assume the test situation has remained constant —in other words, that the level of cohesion has remained more or less the same in each of these villages over the interval between the two administrations of the interview—he can treat the degree of similarity between the scores on the first occasion and on the second as an indication of the reliability of the measure. Let us say the scores of the ten villages for the first and second measurements were as follows:

	First measurement (Test)	Second measurement (Retest)
Village 1	29.3	28.4
Village 2	20.4	19.7
Village 3	31.1	29.9
Village 4	15.7	17.7
Village 5	19.8	20.1
Village 6	26.5	26.6
Village 7	27.2	27.1
Village 8	24.3	23.9
Village 9	23.9	24.2
Village 10	25.4	25.7

These figures reveal substantial consistency of measurement between the two occasions. Almost all the villages had scores on the second measurement occasion that were similar to their scores on the first measurement occasion. Given results such as these, the anthropologist could be rather confident his measure was reliable.[12]

[12] In point of fact, most investigators would not rely on a visual inspection of the two sets of scores to judge the amount of consistency between the two measurement occasions, but would compute a statistic, such as the correlation coefficient, which provides a simple summary indication of the relationship between two sets of scores.

An alternative to the test–retest method of assessing reliability sometimes employed in the case of multi-item research instruments[13] is the *split-half* technique or some variant of it. In this technique, the instrument (often a questionnaire) is divided into two halves, and the degree of consistency between them is ascertained. If the two halves show high consistency with one another this is taken as an indication the measure is reliable.[14]

Still another approach to assessing reliability is sometimes appropriate in anthropological research. Very often a measure employed in an anthropological research situation will involve a considerable amount of interpretation by the researcher or his associates. An example of such a measure would be the following. Suppose an anthropologist is interested in the amount of socialization anxiety in various cultures—that is, the anxiety experienced by a child when he is being taught to give up childish habits and replace them with habits appropriate to older children and adults. This variable might be measured by asking research assistants to read the available ethnographic literature on each culture to be studied and to rate the culture on the variable of socialization anxiety, perhaps by using a seven-point scale indicating low to high anxiety. An anthropologist would be expected to give such assistants rather specific guidelines to follow in making the ratings. He might, for example, tell them to focus on (a) the severity of the punishments used in inducing the child to give up his old habits, (b) the frequency with which a child is punished in this connection, and (c) the amount of emotional distress displayed by the child. The assistants would then base their ratings of socialization anxiety on these three factors.[15]

It is obvious this kind of "interpretive" measure could prove to be very unreliable since individual judgment plays such a large role. One way of gaining information on the reliability of such a measure is to apply the test–retest method we have already discussed. A rater will be asked to rate a number of cultures on socialization anxiety. After sufficient time has passed to reduce the chance of his remembering how he originally rated each culture, he will be given the same materials and asked to rate them a second time. The amount of agreement between his first and second ratings can again be taken as an indication of the *intrarater reliability of the measurement*. A second technique for assessing reliability is also appropriate in such situations. This involves comparison of the ratings of two or more *different* raters. Such a comparison requires that all raters be given the same materials and instructions and that they work independently of each other. If they give similar ratings to the cultures, the measure can be said to possess *high interrater reliability*—consistent results are obtained from the measure when different people employ it. Ideally, an interpretative measure such as the one we have described for socialization anxiety should be shown to have both test–retest reliability and interrater reliability.

Validity   It is not sufficient for a measure merely to be reliable, but reliability

[13] For example, questionnaires or interviews made up of a number of items intended to measure the same variable.

[14] In fact, the split-half procedure, which gives an indication of the *internal* consistency of a measure, taps a rather different component of reliability than does the test–retest approach, which deals with consistency of the measure over repeated applications. For a discussion of this difference, see Cronbach (1967).

[15] This example was inspired by the work of Whiting and Child (1953), although certain details of their procedure have been simplified for this example.

is a prerequisite for establishing whether or not a measure is adequate in terms of our second major criterion—validity. To be valid, *a measure must actually measure the variable we wish to measure and not some other variable.* A thermometer is a valid measure for temperature since it accurately reflects temperature changes. Let us say, however, that we wish to measure humidity instead of temperature. The thermometer would do us little good. Despite its reliability and its validity as a measure of temperature, it is simply not a valid measure of humidity. Humidity could vary greatly while the thermometer reading remained unchanged, or vice versa.

One common approach to establishing the validity of a variable in anthropological research is through the *known-groups technique.* The researcher often has access to two groups he has good reason to believe differ markedly on the variable he wishes to study. He may make use of the "known" difference between these groups to validate his measure—that is, to show that the measure really reflects changes in the variable of interest. Thus, one might reasonably seek to validate a new measure of self-esteem by giving it (a) to a group of men who had just lost an election and (b) to a group composed of winners in the same election. As it is a plausible assumption that the losing group would be lower in self-esteem than the winning group, a valid measure of self-esteem should correctly differentiate these two groups.

An example of the use of the known-groups technique in anthropological research is provided by a study of achievement motivation in Nigeria (Spain 1973). In order to validate a projective measure of achievement motivation,[16] Spain gave the measure to two groups of students. One group was given the measure at a time when they were preparing for a graduation examination which was to be given in one month. This examination was extremely important for their future careers. A second group of students was given the measure fully six months before the time of their graduation examination. It was reasoned that the level of achievement motivation of the first group could be expected to be much higher since studying for the crucial impending examination should have strongly aroused their desire to succeed. The first group did indeed score significantly higher on the measure, and this was taken as evidence supporting the validity of the measure.

A second anthropological example is provided by a study of neighborliness in a rural area of Hong Kong (Brim 1970). Brim gave his questionnaire-type measuring instrument to: (a) residents of a newly erected multistory "resettlement estate" where persons from various cleared squatter areas had been resettled, and (b) residents of several isolated villages. The "resettlement estate" was newly established, in contrast to the long-established villages, and its residents came from very heterogeneous backgrounds. Consequently, Brim reasoned that the estate should exhibit a lower degree of "neighborliness" than the villages. Resettlement estate residents did score markedly lower than the villagers and this was taken as support for the validity of his measure.

---

[16] This measure, originally developed by McClelland and his co-workers (1953), involves showing the informants drawings portraying various activities and asking them to write imaginative stories about them. The stories are scored for achievement motivation according to a scheme developed by McClelland and his associates. See Chapter 3 for several examples of research focusing on achievement motivation.

Sometimes a measure used in research is so obviously connected with the variable to be measured that the investigator feels it unnecessary to establish its validity formally by the known-groups or other methods.[17] Such a measure is sometimes said to possess *face validity*. An example of such a face-valid measure is the method employed by Mischel (1961) in measuring ability to defer gratification. Mischel asked children in a school in Trinidad to fill out questionnaires concerning the structure of their families and certain aspects of their home environments. When each class had finished, he informed the students that in gratitude for their cooperation he wished to give each child a candy bar as a reward. There were two kinds of candy bars available, he said, a large one and a small one. Unfortunately, he did not have enough of the larger bars with him to give one to everyone as he would like. He would be returning to the school the next week, however, and would bring an ample supply of large candy bars then. So he could offer them a choice of a small bar now or a large candy bar of the same quality the following week. If a child chose to receive the small candy bar immediately he was scored as low on ability to defer gratification. If he chose the deferred large candy bar he was scored as high on this ability.

"On the face of it," Mischel's measure appears to be very closely connected to the variable he desired to measure, since it involves actually placing the child in a situation where he can elect either to defer a larger reward or settle for an immediate smaller reward. For this reason the measure can be said to have considerable face validity.

The principle of face validity, it should be pointed out, is subject to abuse. It has too often been relied upon to justify the use of measures whose connection to the variables they purport to measure is "apparent" only to their originators. Moreover, it sometimes happens that a measure which has, by general agreement, a highly "apparent" connection with a variable proves upon further study to be virtually unrelated to that variable.[18] The prospective researcher is thus well advised to be cautious about attempting to establish the validity of measures simply by claiming they have a clear and apparent connection with the variable of interest—that they have "face validity."

At this point, it is appropriate to comment again, for emphasis, on the relationship between reliability and validity. It should be obvious, after some reflection, that reliability is a necessary but not sufficient condition for validity. A measure cannot possess good validity (or "high" validity) if it is intrinsically unstable—if it has low reliability. However, it must also be emphasized that high reliability alone is not an indication of validity. A measure might display excellent stability between measurement occasions and (if applicable) between raters—in other words it might possess excellent test–retest and interrater reliability—but still lack validity. That is to say, it might still be completely unrelated to the variable one desires to measure.

[17] It should be pointed out that there are indeed other ways of validating a measure. Two of the most well known are construct and predictive validity. However, our point here is less a review of validity than it is an illustration of the importance of establishing the validity of a measure. We have chosen to do this in terms of the two more common methods available. The reader interested in further details on the important matter of validity should consult Nunnally (1967).

[18] For a critical discussion of the concept of face validity, see Mosier (1967).

To conclude our discussion of the first two aspects of measurement adequacy, reliability and validity, we can offer the following general observation. The researcher's task is to find measures of his variables that are maximally reliable and valid. He may often find it necessary to make do with measures having only fair reliability and validity, and sometimes he may be unable to assess the measures in these terms at all. However, if given a choice of several different measures of the same variable, he should invariably choose the most valid and reliable.

Precision   A third aspect of a measure's adequacy is its precision. Precision, in this context, refers to the number of distinctions that can be reliably and validly made as to the amount of a variable present when it is measured. There are several ways of classifying measures in terms of their precision. Here, we will distinguish three degrees of precision (in order of increasing precision): categorical, rank-ordering, and quantitative measures.[19]

In *categorical measurement*, the researcher *classifies cases into a small number of categories with respect to the variable of interest.* Some variables seem to be almost inherently categorical. An often used example of such a variable is sex (in the physiological or chromosomal sense); it is generally assumed that, with very rare exceptions, humans fall into only two categories with respect to this variable. More commonly, and often with variables which seem to be inherently categorical, variables in fact represent continua.[20] Nevertheless, the investigator may be forced by the crudity of available measurement operations to treat these continuous variables as though they were categorical. The severity of initiation rites, for example, varies greatly in different cultures. An anthropologist studying the relationship of initiation rites to other cultural variables may be forced, however, by the crudity of his measurement operations and/or the inadequacy of his data, to employ only two categories in the measurement of initiation rite severity—whether initiation rites are present or absent. If there is any indication that a culture has initiation rites of any kind, it will be scored "initiation rites present." Otherwise it will be scored "initiation rites absent."

A great deal of information is obviously lost when categorization is used to measure a variable that is not inherently categorical. It may be very important, for example, to know the relative severity of initiation rites in the various cultures that have such rites. If the researcher is forced to use only the two categories of "present" and "absent" in his measurement such distinctions will be lost since all

---

[19] Although it is similar to several other common measures of precision, the "precision of our measure of measurement precision" is not terribly high. As it stands, it represents a type on the border between categorical and rank-ordering measurement. It compares directly with the widely used four-part classification of measurement: nominal, ordinal, interval, and ratio scales. The first two correspond to the first two in our list; the second two are both types of quantitative measurement. For purposes of our discussion here the distinction between interval and ratio scales is not important and hence we have not used these terms. The reader interested in more details concerning precision of measurement should consult Nunnally (1967).

[20] Indeed, while sex is usually measured in categorical terms ("male" and "female"), it is often the case that researchers are really interested in the more clearly continuous aspects of "sex"—in the maleness and femaleness of an individual's behavior style (defined in specific cultural terms) rather than physiological or chromosomal facts about the individuals being studied.

cultures with initiation rites of any sort—from the least severe to the most severe —will receive the same score on initiation rite severity—"present."

Categorical measurement is commonly encountered in anthropological studies that use raters to make gross estimates of variables on the basis of available ethnographic documents. Often all one can reasonably expect in such a situation is for the raters to be able to sort the cases (usually cultures) into a small number of categories pertaining to the variable of interest, for example, present or absent; or high, medium, low.[21] Finally, it should be emphasized that though categorization represents the weakest form of measurement, it can be highly valuable when more precise forms of measurement are precluded.

Quantitative measurement refers to a situation in which the researcher can *meaningfully assign numbers to the cases to indicate what quantity of the variable they contain.* Some variables can be quantified very easily—for example, population, where numbers are assigned to settlements or other territorial units to indicate the quantity of people they contain. It is more difficult to assign meaningful numbers to represent the quantities of such abstract variables as "respect," "cohesion," or "aggression." Practical techniques have been developed to quantify many such variables, however.[22]

Rank-order measurement falls somewhere between the categorical and quantitative levels of measurement. In rank-order measurement, the investigator is unable to assign a number to each case to represent the quantity of a variable it contains. However, he is able to *rank the cases from highest to lowest in respect to the variable.* Rank-order measurement thus is more informative than simple categorization. However, rank-ordering is substantially inferior to quantitative measurement. Although one may know from a rank-order that case X has more of a particular variable than case Y, one cannot know how *much* more. This difference may be crucial. To give substance to this point, let us examine the rank-ordered list of communities in Table 2.2. We can see from this list that St. Louis has more

TABLE 2.2   COMMUNITIES RANK-ORDERED BY POPULATION

Rank	Name of community
1	San Francisco, California
2	Boston, Massachusetts
3	St. Louis, Missouri
4	Truth or Consequences, New Mexico
5	Republic, Missouri
6	Canal Winchester, Ohio

[21] This illustrates the point just made (in footnote 19) about the arbitrary nature of these distinctions in the precision of measures. It has become traditional to consider a measure that makes such broad distinctions as "high," "medium," and "low" as categorical measures, although in a strict sense they do represent a very weak form of rank-order measurement. We have followed this tradition here.

[22] The following are some of the many sources on measurement in the social sciences that may be examined with profit: Blalock and Blalock (1968), Churchman and Ratoosh (1959), Festinger and Katz (1953), Giselli (1964), Kaplan (1964), Lazarsfeld and Rosenberg (1955), Mehrens and Edel (1967), Pelto (1970), Robinson and Shaver (1969), Selltiz et al. (1951), Senders (1958), and Stouffer (1950).

population than Truth or Consequences, New Mexico. This rank-ordering does not tell us, however, that St. Louis' population (607,718) is more than one hundred times that of Truth or Consequences (4,656), a fact which might be of vital importance for many research questions.

Generally in a research situation one strives to attain the quantitative level of measurement for key variables so as to obtain the maximum possible amount of information. Of course, owing to various practical difficulties, one must sometimes settle for rank-orderings or, as a least-preferred alternative, categorizations.

Replicability

An essential characteristic of science, perhaps the most crucial one, is that *the procedures used to make observations and test hypotheses are described objectively and in detail so that another investigator may repeat and independently verify the results.* This characteristic we may call *replicability.* If the scientific enterprise did not insist on a high level of replicability so as to permit independent verification of results, many erroneous results would find their way into the body of accepted scientific knowledge with potentially disastrous results. One of the most common criticisms of anthropological research in the past has been that the researchers failed to make clear how they arrived at their results, which, of course, precluded replication. In recent years, as the seriousness of the problem has come to be realized, anthropologists have placed increasing emphasis on the objectification of research procedures. It is now more common to find in reports of anthropological research, explicit accounts of how a given result was obtained, including detailed discussion of the measurement procedures used and the way in which a sample of cases was selected. Also, as a result of the increased emphasis on replicability, there has been a tendency for anthropological investigators to move away from reliance on intuition as a basis for measurement (since it is exceedingly difficult to communicate the nature of intuitive processes to another investigator). Rather, there has been a shift toward the use of objective procedures such as standardized tests or observational procedures which can be administered reliably by any trained investigator.

It is difficult to lay down specific rules for maximizing the replicability of one's results, but certain guidelines can be suggested. The investigator should ask himself at each stage of his research whether the procedures he is employing are susceptible to objective description in sufficient detail to permit another trained researcher to repeat them in a comparable situation. If this question cannot be answered affirmatively, it is a strong indication that some rethinking of the operations involved is in order.

The Role of Chance

The competent researcher must constantly be alert to the possibility that the results of a particular research endeavor are the result of chance alone (in other words, that he happened to be "lucky" or "unlucky"). To illustrate this problem, let us consider an imaginary culture where many people experience a type of mental breakdown, lasting only an hour or so, called *zoco*. During a *zoco* attack, a person falls into a trancelike state and appears unable to recognize his relatives and friends. An anthropologist studying this culture forms the hypothesis that *zoco* attacks are the result of "stress" which the individual has experienced. The researcher finds he can devise a test of the hypothesis by taking advantage of the folllowing circumstance. Young people in this culture are required to undergo initiation rites when they reach puberty. Different types of initiation rites, how- ever, are provided for boys and girls. Boys are subjected to a very severe and stressful rite in which they have certain designs cut into their chests, are confronted with terrifying scenes and objects, and are made to prove their competence in athletics, fighting, and other masculine pursuits. In contrast to these highly stressful proceedings, the girls' initiation rites consist of their being taught useful domestic skills, being admonished to be good wives and mothers, and having their faces painted with designs appropriate to adult women.

The initiation ceremonies for the boys represent a rather drastic change in the independent variable of stress, as their effect is to increase greatly the stress experi- enced by the participants. The girls, on the other hand, experience little if any increased stress from their initiation rites. The anthropologist finds he can build a static-group-comparison research design around these ceremonies, using the initiated boys as the treatment group and the initiated girls as the comparison group. Since the number of boys and girls who go through the initiation at any one time is too large to permit him to study all of them, he chooses a sample of boys and girls for study. Because he knows the importance of obtaining a repre- sentative sample, he uses a random means of choosing his sample.[23]

A month after the boys and girls have completed their initiation ceremony, he investigates to see whether any of them have suffered *zoco* attacks during or fol- lowing the ceremonies. This constitutes his measurement, completing the static- group-comparison design that we can diagram as follows:

Treatment group (ten recently initiated boys)	X (boys' stressful initiation cere- mony)	O (whether or not a *zoco* attack occurred)
Control group (ten recently initiated girls)		O (whether or not a *zoco* attack occurred)

Let us suppose that the anthropologist obtained a sample of ten girls and ten boys (in actuality, he would probably try for a considerably larger sample than this) and that the results were as follows:

---

[23] We will discuss more fully the great importance of obtaining a representative sample, and the usefulness of random sampling as a means to this end, in Chapter 4. For the moment, we would note only that obtaining a representative sample is highly desirable *primarily if*, as in the case of the example here, *the researcher wishes to generalize* the results from the sample to a larger population.

	Zoco attacks	No zoco attacks
Treatment group (boys)	6	4
Comparison group (girls)	4	6

The results are certainly consistent with the prediction from the hypothesis. More boys had *zoco* attacks than did girls. Can these results, however, be taken as supporting the hypothesis? The answer must be an emphatic "no," since a result like this could easily occur by chance alone. Let us use an analogy to demonstrate why this is so. Let us say that instead of being interested in the frequency of *zoco* attacks among initiated boys and girls, we are interested in the frequency with which two different coins will come up heads when they are flipped. One coin, let us say, is a silver dollar and the second is a penny. We have a hypothesis, let us imagine, which predicts that the heavier a coin is, the more frequently it will come up heads. Since the silver dollar is by far the heavier, our hypothesis predicts it will come up heads more frequently than will the penny.

Let us flip both coins ten times. If the results were as shown below, would you be inclined to accept the hypothesis that a heavier coin comes up heads more often?

	Tails	Heads
Silver dollar	4	6
Penny	6	4

Probably not, as you no doubt know from experience that it is not unusual for a fair coin (one that is equally likely to come up heads or tails) to show, out of ten flips, six heads due to chance alone. Conversely, it is not unusual for a fair coin to show only four heads out of ten flips, again due to chance variations.

Since we understand the role of chance in coin flipping, we would be reluctant to conclude, on the basis of this evidence, that the hypothesis about the coins was true. We would recognize the possibility that the obtained results, although favorable to the hypothesis, might be due to chance alone and that there was no real relationship between the weight of a coin and its tendency to come up heads when flipped.

It is perhaps less obvious that chance also plays a role in the imaginary study of *zoco* which was described above. To illustrate how chance may enter into the results of research such as this, let us assume that in actuality stress has *no* influence on the frequency of *zoco* attacks and that if the anthropologist had been able to include all the initiated boys and girls in his study he would have obtained the following results:

	Zoco attacks	No zoco attacks
Initiated boys	200	200
Initiated girls	200	200

If in fact the hypothesis is false and, as this table indicates, the boys who undergo great stress in their initiations are no more likely to suffer *zoco* attacks than the unstressed girls, how did it happen that the researcher's results, using the sample of ten boys and ten girls, were consistent with the hypothesis? The explanation is that in randomly selecting boys and girls for the sample, *by chance*, boys who had had *zoco* attacks were somewhat overrepresented in the sample and girls who had had them were underrepresented. We cannot blame the anthropologist for the fact that his sample did not give a correct indication of the actual proportions of boys and girls suffering *zoco* attacks, because he did the best he could to obtain an unbiased sample—that is, he employed random sampling procedures which maximize the chance that a given sample will be representative of the population from which is is drawn. They do not, however, guarantee it. Indeed, as in this example, when random sampling procedures are used there will generally still be some degree of *sampling error*. Sampling error occurs when *the sample is not perfectly representative of the population from which it is drawn*. It is this sampling error—which can make two groups appear to be different when in fact they are not, as in the present example—that may trick an unwary researcher into erroneously concluding that his results support his hypothesis. It is for this reason that the role of chance must be assessed in hypothesis-testing research.

Fortunately, the researcher may avail himself of various statistical techniques that allow him to estimate the effects of chance in a situation such as this. By using these he is able to judge whether his results are likely to be due to chance sampling error alone or whether they indicate that the independent variable (the stressful initiation ceremony here) probably has a real effect on the dependent variable (*zoco* attacks).

It is not within the scope of this book to discuss in detail statistical theory and method. The interested reader may refer to Hardyck and Petrinovich's (1969) excellent introductory book on this topic. He will note there that one statistical procedure which may be applied to the results of this study to estimate the role of chance is the chi-square test (Hardyck and Petrinovich 1969:155 f.). When the chi-square test is applied to our sample results, it indicates that a result this favorable to our hypothesis would result *from chance sampling error alone* more than *one third* of the time. This means that even if there were absolutely no relationship between stress and *zoco* attacks the researcher could still expect to get results that, thanks to sampling error, are as favorable to his hypothesis as these *once out of every three trials!* Clearly, if we accept the anthropologist's *zoco* study results as supporting his hypothesis, we will be running a great risk of mistaking the effects of chance for the effects of the independent variable. Given results such as these, the researcher, if he is prudent, will *not* view them as supporting his hypothesis, even though they seem consistent with it.

He will then have to decide how improbable the rival hypothesis of chance must be before he can reject it as an alternative explanation of the results. Generally, research findings are not accepted as supporting a hypothsis unless, in addition to their being consistent with the hypothesis, the probability of their being due to chance sampling error alone is less than one out of twenty. This one-out-of-twenty criterion is often referred to as the *.05 level of significance*, because .05 is the proportion corresponding to one out of twenty. The chi-square test also indicates that in order to satisfy this criterion, the results in our anthropologist's study would have to favor his hypothesis to at least this degree:[24]

	Zoco *attacks*	No zoco *attacks*
Initiated boys	2	8
Initiated girls	8	2

Conclusion

We have now discussed a number of factors that should be considered in designing hypothesis-testing research in anthropology. On the basis of this material, it is possible to draw up a list of questions that a student of anthropology should ask of any research design. This is true whether the "student" (of whatever status) intends to evaluate his or a colleague's proposed research, or to criticize the published results of hypothesis-testing research. The questions are:

1. Is the research paradigm used the strongest possible one under the circumstances?
2. Do the measurements appear to be satisfactory with regard to their reliability, validity, and precision?
3. Have provisions been made for dealing with the role of chance?
4. Is the execution of the research described in such a way as to be replicable?

If any of these questions cannot be answered affirmatively, there is cause for some concern about the design and, by extension, about the research results that have (or would have) emerged from its use.

[24] When assessing the results of statistical checks against the rival hypothesis of chance, researchers are "*always* confronted with the risk of making one of two types of error" (Selltiz et al. 1959:417, italics added). One type of error, known technically as an "alpha" or "Type I" error, is made when a researcher concludes that there are nonchance differences when in fact there are none. A second type of error, known technically as a "beta" or "Type II" error, is made when a researcher concludes that there are no nonchance differences when in fact there are. It can be seen that there is no way to minimize these two types of errors at the same time because they are "the opposite sides of the same coin." That is, the more we raise the level of significance (for example, by raising the level from .05 to .01) to protect against making Type I errors, the more we open ourselves to Type II errors. Correspondingly, the more we lower our level of significance (for example, by lowering the level from .05 to .10) to protect against making Type II errors, the more we open ourselves to Type I errors. The .05 level of significance we have used here has traditionally been viewed as a compromise between these two types of errors, although there are those who believe this is too strict (that is, by using the .05 level we are making too many Type II errors). In any case, even if the anthropologist's results in this example were such that chance could be ruled out, he would still, of course, have to take into account other rival hypotheses to which his design is subject—in this case, selection and selection interaction effects.

3 / Research design:
Some anthropological
examples

Now that the basic elements of research design have been introduced, we will illustrate their application by turning to examples of research drawn from the literature in anthropology and related fields. This chapter has several interrelated objectives. The primary objective is to elucidate further the strengths and weaknesses of the basic paradigms that were introduced in Chapter 1. In addition, the research reviewed here will illustrate some important techniques that can be used to compensate at least partially for the weaknesses of paradigms such as the static-group-comparison and the pretest–posttest paradigms. This review will also serve to demonstrate that practical measures can be devised for even highly complex and elusive variables of the sort anthropologists must frequently deal with, such as sexual attraction, desire to achieve, tendency to imitate others, and emphasis on compliance in child-training. Finally, this chapter will introduce an important variant of the static-group-comparison paradigm, the "correlational approach."

THE STATIC GROUP COMPARISON IN
ANTHROPOLOGICAL RESEARCH

Coming of Age in Samoa

By far the most common research paradigm in anthropology is the static group comparison. While this paradigm is far from the strongest available, the realities of anthropological research are often such that no stronger designs can be employed. A great deal can be learned from the static group comparison if steps are taken to apply it with maximum effectiveness. As will be seen, this paradigm has been applied by anthropologists in a number of different ways, some of which are clearly superior to others.

Let us begin by considering the least satisfactory variant of the static group comparison. This is a version of the static-group paradigm where one of the two groups is conjectural—that is, either the comparison group or the treatment group has no concrete existence but is instead constructed on the basis of the investigator's general knowledge or intuition. This type of static group comparison is frequently encountered in earlier anthropological works. To illustrate it, let us focus on one classic study—Margaret Mead's *Coming of Age in Samoa* (1928).[1]

The research problem of central importance for Mead in this study concerned the effects of adolescence on children. Many social commentators in Western societies had observed that adolescence was a stormy and crisis-filled period. They hypothesized that this was an inevitable result of the physiological changes occurring at this period in a young person's life. Mead doubted the validity of this hypothesis and countered it with an alternative hypothesis of her own. She suggested that the traumatic nature of adolescence in Western society was not the result of physiological changes in the bodies of adolescents, but was due to the culture in which they lived. In her own words (1928:16), ". . . the question which sent me to Samoa [was]: Are the disturbances which vex our adolescents due to the nature of adolescence itself or to the civilization?" The hypothesis she wished to test, then, may be stated as follows:

INDEPENDENT VARIABLE	NATURE OF RELATIONSHIP	DEPENDENT VARIABLE
Exposure to Western civilization	increases	adolescent trauma.

Mead went to the South Seas island of Samoa to obtain her comparison group. Here she studied a group of adolescent girls who, as they grew up in Samoan culture, enjoyed virtual freedom from the influences of Western culture. Acting as a participant-observer, Mead made highly detailed observations of the emotional and other behavior of a sample of girls. Subsequently, on the basis of these observations, she rated the girls as a group in terms of how much emotional distress they experienced. In her judgment (1928:95), with the exception of a few cases, "adolescence [for these girls] represented no period of crisis or stress, but was instead an orderly developing of a set of slowly maturing interests and activities. The girls' minds were perplexed by no conflicts, troubled by no philosophical queries, beset by no remote ambitions."

Having found a comparison group and having obtained, for the group as a whole, a measure of the dependent variable (adolescent trauma), Mead was faced with the problem of obtaining a treatment group. To do this she resorted to a *conjectural* treatment group. She made no equivalent study of adolescents in West-

---

[1] We select this example because it is beyond question one of the best-known anthropological classics and because, for the period, it represents research of very high quality. We emphasize this last point because it is important for the reader to realize that the deficiencies of this study from the standpoint of research design are not specific to this one work but are representative of anthropological studies undertaken during this period, when, it might be said, the criteria for adequacy of research design had not yet become fully incorporated into the culture of anthropology. It should be pointed out, however, that the anthropology of this time represented a very significant improvement over the pioneering anthropological work of the late nineteenth century, in that it had come to be standard practice for data to be collected by a process of intensive, first-hand participant-observation, rather than being gleaned from the reports of nonanthropological observers, as was the case in much nineteenth-century work.

ern civilization, but instead relied on her general knowledge of a Western society, American society, to construct a treatment group conjecturally. She rated this conjectural group of American adolescents as suffering from a high degree of emotional disturbance, or in her words, "storm and stress." Having supplied a treatment group—albeit a conjectural one—Mead concluded that her hypothesis had been supported. The adolescents in the comparison group, who were isolated from the influence of Western civilization, showed little or no emotional stress at adolescence. The conjectural American adolescent treatment group, which was exposed to Western civilization, did suffer "storm and stress." The results were as predicted by the hypothesis.

We can diagram Mead's study as follows:

Treatment group (conjectural)   (X   O)
   (American adolescent girls)

Comparison group   O
   (Samoan adolescent girls)

In this diagram, the parentheses bracketing the two symbols for the treatment group indicate that the group is conjectural. It is also possible, as has frequently been the case in anthropology, for the comparison group to be conjectural. Such a case would be diagrammed as follows:

Treatment group   X   O

Comparison group (conjectural)   (O)

Here the parentheses bracket the row corresponding to the comparison group to signify that no real cases in this group were actually studied.

Today, we can still admire Mead's study for its many valuable insights into adolescence and for the quality of its description of Samoan culture. The study may also serve as an example of the weaknesses of the version of the static-group-comparison paradigm that employs a conjectural treatment or comparison group. In addition to the weaknesses common to the standard static group comparison, this version of the paradigm contributes a very serious new error source—namely, the imprecision of a conjectural comparison or treatment group. If the investigator does not actually include *both* the treatment and comparison groups in his research, but, as in Mead's study of Samoan girls, relies on general knowledge to conjecture one of the two groups, the possibility of error is greatly magnified. The most serious question raised by such a procedure concerns the equivalence of the measurement procedures for the two groups.

In the present example, Mead based her measurement of emotional stress on extensive, more or less systematic observations of the behavior of a specific group of Samoan adolescent girls. To rate her conjectural American adolescent group, however, she must have relied on a very different body of information, no doubt including her own memories and experiences as an adolescent member of American culture, her subsequent more or less casual observations of American adolescents, and various scholarly studies of American adolescents. She did not make a detailed, systematic behavioral study of a specific group of American adolescents comparable to the one she carried out in Samoa (at least, we are not told if she did). Thus, we are forced to the conclusion that since her ratings of emotional stress for American and Samoan adolescents were based on different sorts of evidence and different measurement procedures, the comparability of the ratings for the two groups of adolescents is compromised.

There is another limitation of Mead's measurement procedure that we should examine—she placed very heavy reliance upon herself as an instrument to measure the variables of interest. Again, we would emphasize that this limitation is not peculiar to Mead's study; rather, it is characteristic of much anthropological research. Mead herself acknowledges this limitation in a statement remarkable (for the time) in its sensitivity to the problem. Regarding her judgment of adolescent emotional stress and the other findings of her study, she notes (1928:153): "The conclusions are . . . all subject to the limitation of the personal equation. They are the judgments of one individual upon a mass of data, many of the most significant aspects of which can, by their very nature, be known only to herself."

In a test of a hypothesis, exclusive reliance on the personal judgment of the researcher as the means of measuring key variables is undesirable. Experience has shown that a person's judgment of a situation can be markedly affected by his expectations—that is, a person tends to see in a situation what he expects to see, even if it is not objectively present (see, for example, Rosenthal 1966). Complete reliance on this sort of judgmental measurement by the anthropologist can introduce considerable measurement error. Not only is there some danger of the anthropologist unconsciously "misjudging" various behaviors, but he may also, again quite unconsciously, tend to be somewhat selective in his observations, being particularly alert to behavior that conforms to his expectations and tending to overlook other behavior he does not expect. This is *not* to say that all anthropological observations are inaccurate, but does point up the serious possibility of substantial measurement error which may result from unconscious distortion and/or selection of the data on the part of the anthropologist who relies so heavily on judgments of this type.

The problem of unconscious observer bias can be ameliorated somewhat if the data collected by the anthropologist are rated by independent judges who are not aware of the hypothesis being tested. Also, if several independent judges are used, an estimate of the interrater reliability of the rating system can be obtained. This approach still does not completely eliminate the problem of inadvertent selection of behavior that favors the hypothesis, however, since we are still dependent on the anthropologist himself to observe and record a behavior sample to serve as a basis for ratings.

This problem has not been ignored by anthropologists. In recent years, as they have come to recognize the serious consequences stemming from misjudgment of data and unconscious data selection, there has been a move toward supplementing participant-observation by using more objective data-collection instruments. These devices and procedures include standardized interview protocols and schedules, questionnaires, projective tests, and regularized procedures for sampling and recording behavior which reduce the possibility that an anthropologist's expectations may unconsciously affect his reporting of the data.

But Mead's study is not only weakened by measurement problems. Even if we assume that Mead's conjectures regarding the treatment group were accurate and her measurements of the Samoan comparison group were valid, there are other sources of possible error. For example, as was pointed out in Chapter 1, the static-group-comparison paradigm guards against the effects of extraneous variables only to the extent that the treatment and comparison groups are affected by these variables in the same manner. If there is an interaction between selection and the effects of extraneous variables, that is, if the cases in the treatment and comparison groups are differently affected by extraneous variables, there is a very real danger that an observed difference between the two groups in regard to the dependent variable may be due to one or several of these extraneous factors and may have no connection with the independent variable. It is possible to identify several factors (extraneous variables) that might differentially affect Mead's treatment and control groups and might therefore be responsible for the difference in amount of observed emotional stress.

For example, the genetic makeup of the two groups of adolescents being compared is obviously different. There are strong indications that there are important genetic components in psychological factors such as emotionality (Eysenck and Prell 1951). It is therefore possible the Samoan adolescents were constitutionally less subject to emotional stress. Another possibility is that the tropical illnesses to which Samoan teenagers were subject had the effect of making them somewhat listless and therefore less subject to emotional arousal. These two alternative hypotheses cannot be ruled out, since the factors involved in them cannot be controlled by Mead's application of the conjectural static group comparison; in other words, it cannot be assumed that these factors affect both groups equally.

A static group comparison can be greatly strengthened by selecting treatment and comparison groups that resemble each other as much as possible and that are likely therefore to be affected by extraneous factors in nearly the same manner.[2] When dealing with a hypothesis such as Mead's, there is little possibility of obtaining comparison and treatment groups that are similar in regard to the major extraneous variables. It would almost certainly be futile, for example, to try and locate

---

[2] The goal of selecting societies or cultures for study that are similar in virtually every way except for the one issue or variable of interest is the core of what is known in anthropology as the "method of controlled comparison." Eggan's discussion of this method is one of the most thorough and widely known (Eggan 1954); Nadel's study of witchcraft in four African societies is perhaps the most famous anthropological application of this method (Nadel 1952). Although seldom explained in these terms, the effect of such a method of sample selection is to reduce the likelihood that extraneous variables will affect the two groups differently and in this way protect against a serious rival hypothesis. Such a procedure is desirable when using this method because a "controlled comparison" is essentially the same as a static-group-comparison paradigm. And, as we have noted, the problem of extraneous variables with this paradigm can be minimized if the groups compared can be assumed to have responded similarly to them; this assumption is more tenable if the groups are similar. Unfortunately, however, most instances where this method has been employed by anthropologists have been for the comparison of relatively few cultures or societies (often as few as two) and this has meant that it was impossible to consider the role of chance.

a non-Western cultural group that has the same genetic makeup and the same diet as a Western cultural group. In the case of many other, more specific, hypotheses, however, it *is* possible to locate similar treatment and comparison groups. For an example of this, let us return to Mead's study.

Mead realized that even if she were able to demonstrate conclusively that Western cultures produced a high degree of adolescent emotional stress, such a conclusion would be of limited practical value since it would provide no indication of what specific cultural institutions might be changed in order to improve the lot of adolescents. She therefore went on to develop some relatively specific hypotheses relating particular cultural features to adolescent distress. She suggested, for example, that when multiple standards of sexual morality are found in a culture (as in American culture) an adolescent is placed under increased stress, since he or she faces the dilemma of which standard to adopt. Samoan culture, Mead suggests, has in effect only one standard of sexual morality. This makes it possible to develop a more specific and potentially more useful hypothesis that can be diagrammed as follows:

INDEPENDENT VARIABLE	NATURE OF RELATIONSHIP	DEPENDENT VARIABLE
Being subjected to competing standards of sexual morality	increases	emotional distress at adolescence.

As we have seen, an attempt to test this hypothesis using a static group comparison between groups that are as different as American and Samoan adolescents runs up against perhaps insurmountable difficulties in that there are many *uncontrolled extraneous variables* (variables which will affect the two groups differently) whose effects can masquerade as those of the independent variable. A more powerful test of this hypothesis might be carried out by selecting for a static group comparison two groups of girls drawn from the *same* culture but differing in the extent to which they are exposed to competing standards of morality. Since both groups would be drawn from the same culture, the problem of extraneous variables would be considerably reduced as the groups would be affected in the same way by many, if not most, extraneous factors. Mead herself pointed out that such a comparison would have been possible in her research setting, since some of the girls went to live in the households of native pastors where they were exposed to moral standards very different from those which they had learned in their own families (1928:155).

In summary, employing the criteria for evaluating a research design that we proposed at the conclusion of Chapter 2, Mead's study can be criticized on at least five grounds. First, the paradigm she used was not the strongest possible under the circumstances. She could at least have utilized the standard static group comparison instead of the inferior conjectural version of the static group comparison. Second, the reliability of the measurements is seriously in doubt due to the facts that (a) the researcher used herself as a measuring instrument for adolescent stress, apparently by a primarily intuitive process, and (b) no direct measurements were made on the treatment group—a group which was essentially conjectural. Third, the validity of the measurements is seriously in doubt for the same reasons given regarding the reliability of the measures. Fourth, the replicability of the design is seriously deficient, again largely because of the subjective nature of the measurement process. And fifth, the absence of an actual treatment group made it impossible to apply statistical tests to take into account the role of chance.

Child Marriage in Taiwan

In the discussion of Margaret Mead's *Coming of Age in Samoa*, it was suggested that it is possible to strengthen a static group comparison considerably by obtaining treatment and comparison groups which are as similar as possible. This strengthens the paradigm because, in general, the more similar two groups are, the greater the likelihood that they will be exposed to the same extraneous variables. A study which illustrates this principle is Wolf's examination (Wolf 1970) of Westermarck's hypothesis (Westermarck 1926) that childhood association produces "sexual aversion"—in other words, that a boy and girl who are in close association with one another from infancy will develop no sexual interest in one another and indeed may actively feel repulsed by thought of sexual contact. Wolf did fieldwork in an area of Taiwan where the existence of two contrasting types of marriage made it possible to construct a static-group-comparison test of the Westermarck hypothesis. In one type of marriage, which Wolf calls the "minor" form of marriage, the bride-to-be comes into her future husband's household as an infant or small child. She is "adopted" by her future husband's parents and reared together with him until they both reach maturity, at which time their marriage is finalized. In the second type of marriage, called the "major" form of marriage by Wolf, the bride and groom typically do not meet until the time of their marriage, when they are both adults.

As we have noted, Westermarck's hypothesis predicts that intimate childhood association between a boy and girl will result in their having no sexual attraction for one another. The relationship of the variables in this hypothesis may be stated as follows:

INDEPENDENT VARIABLE	NATURE OF RELATIONSHIP	DEPENDENT VARIABLE
Close childhood association	decreases	sexual attraction.

Individuals in "minor" marriages can be considered as cases in a treatment group in regard to this hypothesis since they have grown up in intimate association with their spouse. Individuals in the "major" marriage form provide a comparison group since they have experienced no childhood association with their spouses.

Wolf was able to devise several measures of the dependent variable of sexual attraction. He assumed the number of children produced by a marriage was directly related to sexual attraction between husband and wife. That is, couples who attract one another sexually produce more children than those who are not attracted to one another sexually. He also assumed that if a marriage ended in divorce or featured adultery involving the wife, this was usually an indication of a low degree of sexual attraction.

Wolf's study may be diagrammed as follows:

Treatment group (couples in minor marriages)	X (childhood association)	O (number of children and outcome of marriage)
Comparison group (couples in major marriages)		O (number of children and outcome of marriage)

The results of this comparison, shown in Tables 3.1 and 3.2, were consistent with the Westermarck hypothesis. Minor marriages showed a much higher incidence of divorce and/or adultery by the wife. Wives in minor marriages also had substantially fewer children.

TABLE 3.1   NUMBER AND PERCENT OF MARRIAGES ENDING IN DIVORCE AND/OR INVOLVING ADULTERY BY WIFE[a]

	Minor marriage	Major marriage
Total number of marriages	132	171
Number involving divorce and/or adultery	61	18
Percent involving divorce and/or adultery	46.2	10.5

[a] From Wolf 1970:512, Table 5. Reproduced by permission of the American Anthropological Assn. from the *American Anthropologist*, 72(3), 1970.

TABLE 3.2   AVERAGE NUMBER OF CHILDREN AS TAKEN FROM HOUSEHOLD REGISTRATION RECORDS[a]

Years of marriage (in five-year intervals)	Minor marriage	Major marriage
1st	1.27	1.81
2nd	1.19	1.62
3rd	1.12	1.54
4th	1.06	1.23
5th	0.54	0.75

[a] From Wolf 1970:512, Table 6. Reproduced by permission of the American Anthropological Assn. from the *American Anthropologist*, 72(3), 1970.

Because Wolf obtained his comparison and treatment groups from the same culture instead of from two different cultures (indeed, the groups were both obtained from a single small region in Taiwan) he could reasonably assume that many extraneous factors were the same for both groups. This was not, however, true for all extraneous factors. Importantly, the two groups were exposed to different levels of the extraneous variables of socioeconomic status and adoption. These differences were important because they led to rival hypotheses that might have accounted for the different scores of the groups on the dependent variable.

It could be suggested, for example, that because women in minor marriages were all adopted in infancy this might in itself have been responsible for the smaller number of children resulting from minor marriages. There is some reason to believe that women adopted in this fashion were often mistreated by their foster parents and perhaps did not eat as well as the other members of their adoptive families. Deprivation experienced by such women in their childhoods could have lowered their fertility and caused them to bear fewer children when they married.

Minor marriages also are generally entered into by persons of low socioeconomic standing. This factor might in itself have led to the high rates of divorce and adultery observed for minor marriages. Women, for example, might have been motivated by extreme poverty to leave their husbands in search of a more materially rewarding life situation. Men might have been more likely to desert their wives in order to escape the burden of providing for a family. It might also be suggested that persons of low status may have different standards regarding divorce and extramarital sex. If these standards were more permissive, this in itself could account for the higher incidence of both of these phenomena. The poverty that accompanied low status might also have been responsible for the lower fertility of women in minor marriages, since poor health tends to accompany poverty.

If unrefuted, these rival hypotheses, which follow from the differences between the treatment and comparison groups on the two extraneous factors of adoption and social status, would throw into serious doubt the conclusion that the results of the study support the Westermarck hypothesis. However, Wolf was able to make a strong case that social status and adoption differences were not responsible for the differences in scores on the dependent variable. He did this by matching couples from the major and minor marriage groups on the two extraneous variables. In other words, he selected cases that were equal in terms of these extraneous variables. There were, he found, forty-two women in the major marriage group who had been reared as adopted daughters in preparation for minor marriages. Because of the death of their intended spouses or other circumstances, these women had married in the major form instead. They had, however, been exposed to the effects of adoption, just as were the women who went ahead with minor marriages. They were also, by and large, from the same socioeconomic stratum as the minor marriage wives.

Wolf carried out a new static group comparison. This time, he compared two groups of women—those forty-two who had been "adopted" for minor marriage but had ended up in major marriages, and those who had been "adopted" and did enter minor marriage as planned. In this comparison the effects of the two extraneous variables of status and adoption were essentially controlled since both the treatment group and the new comparison group were affected by them to approximately the same extent. Thus, these two extraneous variables could not account for any differences between the two groups regarding their scores on the dependent variable. This new comparison is diagrammed below:

Treatment group (couples in minor marriages)	X (childhood association)	O (number of children and outcome of marriage)
Comparison group (couples in major marriages where the wife was reared as an adopted daughter-in-law in preparation for a minor marriage)		O (number of children and outcome of marriage)

The results of this new comparison were very similar to those of the original comparison. Again, the treatment group of minor marriages, where husband and wife were reared together, produced fewer children and featured much higher rates of divorce and/or adultery involving the wife (see Tables 3.3 and 3.4).

TABLE 3.3   NUMBER AND PERCENT OF MARRIAGES BY ADOPTED DAUGHTERS ENDING IN DIVORCE AND/OR INVOLVING ADULTERY BY WIFE[a]

	Minor marriage	Major marriage
Total number of marriages	132	42
Number ending in divorce	25	1
Number ending in adultery	42	4
Percent involving divorce and/or adultery	46.2	9.5

[a] From Wolf 1970:514, Table 8. Reproduced by permission of the American Anthropological Assn. from the *American Anthropologist*, 72(3), 1970.

TABLE 3.4   AVERAGE NUMBER OF CHILDREN BY ADOPTED DAUGHTERS AS TAKEN FROM HOUSEHOLD REGISTRATION RECORDS[a]

Years of marriage (in five-year intervals)	Minor marriage	Major marriage
1st	1.27	1.78
2d	1.19	1.77
3d	1.12	1.76
4th	1.06	1.31
5th	0.54	0.90

[a] From Wolf 1970:514, Table 9. Reproduced by permission of the American Anthropological Assn. from the *American Anthropologist*, 72(3), 1970.

Since status and adoption have been effectively ruled out as rival hypotheses accounting for the observed difference in the two groups' scores on the measures of the dependent variables, Wolf was in a much stronger position when he suggested that these results support Westermarck's hypothesis that prolonged and intimate childhood association decreases sexual attractiveness.[3]

It is likely that the two groups in Wolf's study were differentially affected by at least some extraneous variables other than the two he dealt with by matching. It is not easy, however, to suggest any that might plausibly be held to affect the dependent variable. Nonetheless, Wolf's conclusions may be thrown into contention if he himself or some other researcher is subsequently able to suggest such an extraneous variable.

It is important to note that selection seems to pose little problem in Wolf's research, even though he is using a paradigm which is vulnerable to error from this source. A primary danger in many applications of the static group comparison, as we have seen, is that as a result of selection, the treatment group will already be high (or low) on the dependent variable by the time it is exposed to the independent variable. In such a situation the effect of selection can masquerade as that of the independent variable and lead the researcher into a false inference. This possibility seems remote here, since the research situation is one in which the independent variable, childhood association, typically begins to act not long after birth. It is hard to imagine in what way selection effects could cause the two groups compared to differ on the dependent variable of sexual interest *prior* to the onset of the independent variable. Since much anthropological research deals with independent variables that have an early onset, such as the one here, it is often the case that preexisting differences on the dependent variable due to selection can be discounted as a possible rival hypothesis. (Effects of selection may often continue to be a problem, however. See, for example, the selection-related problem discussed for LeVine's study, pages 42–48.)

Evaluating Wolf's research design according to the general criteria we developed in Chapter 2, we can say the following: The paradigm used is the strongest possible one under the circumstances and has been strengthened substantially by Wolf's efforts to control extraneous variables through the procedure of matching cases. Regarding reliability, two of the measures he employed—the number of children a woman gave birth to and the occurrence of divorce—were taken from population records, which, presumably, were carefully maintained. These data are probably reliable as there is relatively little chance of the researcher misjudging data of this sort. Of course, further evidence of the accuracy of the original documentary records would be desirable. Wolf's information on adultery on the part of wives is perhaps open to question from the standpoint of reliability, in part because his sources for this information were "well-informed" local informants. No interrater reliability checks were reported. (The sensitive nature of the topic probably made it difficult

---

[3] Campbell and Stanley (1966) point out that in some situations matching can introduce serious error due to a statistical artifact known as "regression," although this does not appear to pose a problem in Wolf's research. Such error may be avoided by use of a type of statistical analysis known as analysis of covariance, which achieves the benefits of matching without the risk of error due to regression (cf. Campbell and Stanley 1966:15–16, 49–50, 70–71; Thorndike 1942).

to do the extensive cross-checking needed to establish interrater reliability for this information.) Wolf, however, argues that these data may very well be reliable because his two principal informants "are old enough to have known all of the women in the sample in their youth and are attuned to local gossip because they are often called upon to act as mediators and go-betweens" (1970:510). In any case, Wolf's conclusions do not rest on this index alone since he is able to support it with the other two kinds of information already discussed.

Wolf's measures possess a compelling amount of face validity. It is reasonable to expect that fertility, divorce, and adultery are all to some extent functions of sexual attraction, although, to be sure, each may reflect other factors as well. Our intuitive confidence in the validity of these three measures is further strengthened by the fact that all three indicators are consistent with one another, as they would be expected to be if they are all measuring the same underlying trait of sexual attraction. Once again, however, more formal evidence of the validity of these indicators as measures of sexual attraction would be highly desirable, but given the very sensitive nature of the subject, formal validation procedures would no doubt be difficult to arrange.

The replicability of the study is high. Wolf clearly describes how the various measurements were obtained and the nature of the sample he worked with. Although Wolf unfortunately does not apply statistical procedures to obtain an estimate of the role of chance, it appears from the summary data he has provided that conventional tests of significance would show that the possibility of the differences between the two groups being due to chance alone is extremely small.

Achievement in Nigeria

Wolf's research illustrates one way in which a static group comparison can be strengthened—that is, by controlling confounding extraneous variables through matching of cases. Another way of dealing with extraneous variables in a static group comparison is illustrated in research carried out in Nigeria by LeVine (1966). LeVine's study concerns achievement motivation, a motive that may be defined as a desire to succeed in terms of some objective standard of excellence. Achievement motivation appears (McClelland 1961) to be an important factor affecting rates of economic growth. As a consequence, there has been considerable interest in discovering factors that produce variation in the amount of achievement motivation possessed by different individuals and in the average amounts of achievement motivation found in different societies.

LeVine has hypothesized that achievement motivation will be affected by the kind of "status mobility system" in the society in which one lives. Since achievement motivation is essentially a deep-seated concern with being successful according to, or in terms of, some objective standard of excellence, he reasoned that cultures which, by virtue of their social organization, permitted people to rise in accordance with their ability to compete successfully with an objective standard, would also be cultures where people tended to have high achievement motivation. Accordingly, and in view of evidence from other research showing a relationship between an interest in business success and high levels of achievement motivation, LeVine hypothesized that societies in which upward mobility was achieved primarily as a result of one's ability in a pecuniary or occupational endeavor would have higher levels of achievement motivation than would societies in which success in the political arena was stressed. LeVine's independent variable may be termed the "pecuniary-ness" of the status mobility system.[4] The basic hypothesis may be diagrammed as follows:

INDEPENDENT VARIABLE	NATURE OF RELATIONSHIP	DEPENDENT VARIABLE
"Pecuniary-ness" of the status mobility system in a culture	increases	achievement motivation among persons in that culture.

A measure of the dependent variable, achievement motivation, was obtained by asking informants, who were male students in secondary schools, to write essays describing dreams they had had. These dream reports were then scored for imagery indicative of strong motivation to achieve.[5] An example of a dream description judged as containing achievement imagery is the following:

From my childhood, I have been dreaming dreams but there is one particular dream which I dream often. Probably I may dream about it this night. The dream is in fact very simple but quite funny. Whenever I dream, I see myself as Albert Onyeonwuna, the Nigerian international footballer.

I saw myself as Albert Onyeonwuna being made the captain of Nigerian team in a football-soccer competition against Ghana. I dreamt that this match was played at Lagos stadium and that the Nigerian "Red Devils," with me as captain, defeated Ghana "Iron Gates" by two goals to nil. The match was played on a rainy day and the slippery ground added fun to what could be described as the most exciting match ever played in Nigeria.

Both teams started at a fast pace and with grim determination so that it was difficult to choose between the two. Suddenly I, as Onyeonwuna, came into the picture. I dashed for the ball and after beating Ghana's right fullback, sent in a fiery shot which left Ghana's goalkeeper sprawling on the ground. The people who were in the stadium jumped up from their seats in anxiety and started clapping their hands. From that time, there were anxious moments whenever I was in possession of the ball, for the people wanted me to score more goals. The applause had hardly died down when I received a short pass from our inside right winger, Emuke. I stopped the ball, and after beating Ghana's right halfback man, parcelled the ball with a short trip to our man in the centre forward. He was in the position to kick the ball when he was kicked down by the Ghana fullback man, and this attracted the referee for a penalty kick. I was the person who played the penalty kick and it was a clean goal. Thus I raised the goal tally for our team to two. We had only two minutes to go in the match

---

[4] The reasoning behind this hypothesis is complex and is related to general theory about achievement motivation. Without going into details, it may be noted that LeVine sees child training as the efficient cause of *n* Achievement and therefore the "pecuniary-ness" of the status mobility system only indirectly affects achievement by means of its impact on child-training practices. The reader interested in these issues should consult LeVine's clearly written discussion (1966). We have elected also to minimize LeVine's discussion of data collected from a third group, the Yoruba. These data support LeVine's hypothesis, but to discuss them in detail here would deflect us from the more central issue of the research design LeVine used. Some of the Yoruba data, however, are introduced later on in this discussion to illustrate other characteristics of LeVine's research design.

[5] See LeVine 1966:103 ff. for details of the scoring system.

and Ghana players, now tired and playing short of one man, were forced into a defensive game; thus we maintained the lead of two nil until the final whistle.

This is, in fact, the dream I dream most, and whenever I wake up the following morning, I become unhappy for I realize that I am not Onyeonwuna, but Alozie.[6]

An example of a dream description judged to lack achievement imagery is this one:

There is a certain dream which I cannot sleep for a month without dreaming of it since about two years now.

I have several times seen myself flying like birds in a dream. The first day I dreamt the dream, I was going to a certain place and I was attacked by a dangerous animal. To my surprise, I flew away and the animal could not harm me, as it did not know how to fly.

On one other day I was in a dream, there was something like war. An aeroplane was flying through our town and people were shouting that the enemies had come to throw bombs. I took a kind of gun and flew away. After I had gone up to a certain height, I shot the aeroplane down and there was no effect. Then we defeated our enemies.

In fact I have always seen myself flying like birds in a dream that I do not take notice of it again because it is almost constant. Whenever in my dream I have encountered any danger, I fly away like birds from the ground to the air.[6]

LeVine was able to devise a static-group-comparison test of his hypothesis by collecting data from cultures with status mobility systems which differed traditionally in respect to the relevance of pecuniary as opposed to political success. One of the cultures LeVine chose for study was Igbo culture. The Igbo reside in eastern Nigeria and traditionally featured a mobility system where it was possible for an individual to greatly increase his status by competing with others in regard to an objective standard of success—namely, through individual achievement in commercial or other pecuniary activity. A second culture studied by LeVine was Hausa culture, where traditionally it was not generally possible for a man to achieve high status by means of individual pecuniary achievement. Instead, in Hausa culture a person could rise only through clientage—that is through a relationship of diffuse loyalty and obedience to a person of high status who was or might become a powerful officeholder in the political arena.

The static group comparison LeVine devised using groups of informants drawn from these two cultures may be diagrammed as follows:

Igbo students (exposed to a pecuniarily oriented status mobility system)	X (exposure to pecuniarily oriented status mobility system)	O
Hausa students (not exposed to a pecuniarily oriented status mobility system)		O

In comparing the frequency of achievement themes in stories written by the students from the pecuniarily oriented Igbo culture to that in stories by students from the politically oriented Hausa culture, LeVine found, as predicted by his hypothesis, that the former group had more achievement themes—43 percent as compared to 17 percent. A statistical test indicated that a difference of this magnitude could be expected to occur by chance alone less than one time in one thousand. LeVine was thus able to dispose of the rival hypothesis of chance. However, at this point he still had to contend with a number of other rival hypotheses.

Due to the nature of the research situation, the treatment and comparison groups, which were drawn from different cultures, were unavoidably affected in different ways by a number of extraneous variables, some of which produced plausible rival hypotheses. One such rival hypothesis was that the difference in achievement motivation between the groups might have been due to a religious factor. The Igbo treatment group was overwhelmingly Protestant Christian in religion, while the Hausa comparison group was predominantly Moslem. It might conceivably be maintained that Protestant Christianity is a religion which encourages individual achievement, while Islam lays more stress on obedience, thereby discouraging individual achievement, and that this difference in the two groups' religious orientation suffices to explain their differences in achievement motivation.

LeVine dealt with this rival hypothesis in the following manner. He had, as part of his study, collected information on a group of students from a third culture in Nigeria—the Northern Yoruba. It happens that some Northern Yoruba are Christian and some are Moslem. LeVine reasoned that if exposure to Protestantism, as opposed to Islam, was a factor in determining level of achievement motivation, it should be possible to demonstrate this by means of a static group comparison of Christian Northern Yoruba and Moslem Northern Yoruba. This comparison may be diagrammed as follows:

Christian Northern Yoruba   X   O

                         (exposure to
                          Protestant
                          Christianity)

_____

Moslem Northern Yoruba   O

The results of this static group comparison revealed absolutely no indication that Protestant Christianity promoted achievement motivation any more than did Islam (Table 3.5). LeVine inferred from this result that it was improbable that the

TABLE 3.5   PERCENTAGE OF AI[a] DREAMERS AMONG THE NORTHERN
YORUBA ACCORDING TO RELIGIOUS AFFILIATION[b]

	Moslem	Christian	Totals
AI	27.2(3)	27.2(6)	9
Non-AI	72.8(8)	72.8(16)	24
Totals	100 (11)	100 (22)	33

[a] AI = Achievement Imagery.
[b] Adapted from LeVine, 1966:59, Table 5. Copyright © 1966, University of Chicago Press and used with permission.

difference in achievement motivation between the Igbo and the Hausa could be the result of the extraneous factor of religious differences. He therefore rejected this rival hypothesis. (But see p. 47 for a cautionary note.)

A second rival hypothesis was related to the fact that the parents of the Igbo informants had generally received much more Western education than had those of the Hausa. It could be hypothesized that this extraneous factor was capable of accounting for the difference in achievement motivation between the two groups. A rationale for such a hypothesis might be that Western education stresses individual achievement. Therefore, if a child's parents were Western educated, it is likely they would give more stress to achievement in their training of the child.

LeVine was able to discredit this rival hypothesis in a manner analogous to his procedure regarding the rival hypothesis involving religion. He found that there was enough variability in terms of parental education within the group of Igbo informants to permit a static-group-comparison test of the hypothesis that having Western-educated parents would increase achievement motivation. Igbo boys who had mothers[7] with little or no Western education were compared with those whose mothers had substantial Western education; that is:

Igbos with mothers having substantial Western education	X (exposure to a mother with substantial Western education)	O
Igbos with mothers having little or no Western education		O

This static group comparison showed that having a Western-educated mother had no appreciable effect (Table 3.6). LeVine therefore dismissed as improbable the rival hypothesis of parental education.

Finally, by following a procedure analogous to that described for the two rival hypotheses treated above, LeVine also was able to reject as improbable a third rival hypothesis which involved special drive-arousing circumstances affecting the Hausa but not the Igbo.

The technique of discounting rival hypotheses used by LeVine—testing the rival hypothesis in a different situation and showing it to be unsupported in that situation—can be referred to as "control by testing." Control by testing is generally less powerful than control by matching,[8] which we discussed in connection with Wolf's study. This is the case because showing that a factor has no effect in one situation

---

[7] LeVine compared the boys in terms of their mothers' education rather than their fathers' education or fathers' and mothers' combined education on the grounds that the mother's education was ". . . theoretically the most powerful influence on personality development, since the mother has the most contact with the child . . ." (1966:57).

[8] We use "control by matching" to refer both to the actual matching of cases and to the statistical counterparts of matching such as covariance analysis and partial correlation.

TABLE 3.6 MOTHERS' EDUCATION AND PERCENTAGE OF SONS REPORTING
ACHIEVEMENT IMAGERY DREAMS[a]

	Percent reporting dreams with achievement imagery	Percent reporting dreams without achievement imagery
Igbos with mothers having up through five years of Western education	45(46)[b]	55(56)
Igbos with mothers having more than five years of Western education	43(15)	57(20)

[a] Adapted from LeVine 1966:58, Table 4. Copyright © 1966 University of Chicago Press. Used by permission.
[b] Numbers in parentheses are numbers of informants.

does not guarantee it will have no effect in a different situation. Thus, showing that Protestant Christianity as opposed to Islam has no effect on achievement among the Northern Yoruba does not guarantee religion did not cause a difference in achievement motivation between the Igbo and the Hausa. Similarly, showing that mother's education does not influence achievement motivation within the Igbo group does not guarantee that this factor does not contribute to the difference in achievement motivation between the Igbo and the Hausa. Demonstrations such as these, however, do *reduce* the likelihood that the extraneous factors involved are important determinants of the dependent variable. Thus, control by testing is well worth applying when control by matching is impossible.

LeVine also identified but was unable to positively reject several other rival hypotheses deriving from extraneous variables that may have affected the two groups in different ways. One of these concerned population pressure. The Igbo are subject to extreme population pressure on limited land resources. The Hausa experience substantially less population pressure. It might be argued that the high population pressure in Igbo-occupied areas and the attendant threat of poverty could give rise to a high level of motivation to achieve, especially in regard to commercial and other nonagricultural activities. LeVine argues against this and two additional rival hypotheses, but is unable to dismiss them since neither control by matching nor control by testing could be applied to the extraneous factors involved, given the limitations of the particular research situation. Thus, these hypotheses remain as untested but reasonable alternatives to the status mobility system hypothesis advocated by LeVine. Though such results might seem at first to be cause for discouragement, they are for LeVine (as for others familiar with the nature of scientific inquiry) a stimulus for research. LeVine concludes his study by urging the design of further research that will take into account these alternative hypotheses.

Selection also posed a problem in LeVine's study, since the several schools from which LeVine's student informants were drawn varied considerably in their entrance requirements. The entrance requirements for the government colleges (which, as LeVine suggests, "are universally regarded as the schools with the best students") are lower in the northern part of Nigeria where the Hausa are concentrated than they are elsewhere in the country. Thus, it could be argued that the Hausa students are "likely to be of lower caliber than their Ibo [sic] counterparts" (1966:45). If this is true, and if "lower caliber" implies (among other things) a lower degree of achievement motivation, selection becomes a plausible rival hypothesis explaining the difference between the Hausa and Igbo. LeVine suggests that selection bias due to the government colleges' differing entrance requirements may be offset by other circumstances relating to selection of the sample. And so, while he is not able to rule out selection as a rival hypothesis, he discounts it on the grounds that when these other factors are considered, "there is no convincing evidence that the selection of subjects biased the results . . . (1966:46)."

We can assess LeVine's study in terms of our general evaluative criteria as follows. The paradigm chosen for the study, the static group comparison, appears to be the most powerful that is feasible, given the nature of the research problem. A more powerful paradigm such as the nonequivalent-control-group paradigm or the standard-control-group paradigm would require premeasurement of the dependent variable. But this is unfeasible since, as was the case in Wolf's study, the independent variable begins to act in early childhood, if not in infancy. The study attains a high level of replicability since all stages of the research and the various procedures employed are explained in detail (for example, LeVine includes an appendix describing the scoring of dream reports for achievement motivation). Both intrarater and interrater reliabilities are provided for the scorings of the dream reports, and they prove to be satisfactorily high. There is no formal demonstration of validity for the dream measure of achievement motivation. However, the measure was closely patterned after another technique for measuring achievement motivation that has been shown to be valid (see McClelland et al. 1953). The dream descriptions also were scored by raters who knew nothing of the hypothesis of the study, eliminating another potentially invalidating factor. The role of chance was taken into account by application of appropriate statistical tests, and this procedure indicated that the rival hypothesis of chance could be conclusively rejected.

To conclude our discussion of LeVine's study we may note that LeVine has been able to strengthen greatly the case for his hypothesis relating type of status mobility system to achievement motivation, although he has *not* been able to reject *all* rival hypotheses. While some plausible rival hypotheses remain unrefuted by this study, it is to be hoped that future research in different settings will be successful in testing them. If this is done and the rival hypotheses that LeVine was unable to deal with are shown to be invalid, the case for LeVine's hypothesis will be still stronger.

Child-training and Food Accumulation

Many hypotheses of interest to anthropologists cannot be tested within a single culture because they deal with factors that do not vary sufficiently within such relatively limited bounds. For example, hypotheses concerning type of descent system can seldom be tested within the confines of a single culture since cultures tend to be homogeneous with regard to this variable—that is, all (or virtually all) Chinese reckon kinship patrilineally, all Trobrianders reckon kinship matrilineally, and so on. Testing hypotheses involving such variables generally requires a cross-cultural approach—in other words, information must be gathered from more than one culture. LeVine's study, which we have just discussed, provides one example of the cross-cultural approach. Since LeVine wanted to test a hypothesis concerning the effects of a culture's status mobility system on individuals' achievement motivation, and since a status mobility system is more or less uniform within a particular culture, he found it necessary to use informants drawn from two cultures in order to obtain treatment and comparison groups that were exposed to sufficiently differing degrees of the independent variable. The cases in LeVine's research were still individuals, even though the two groups of individuals being compared were drawn from different cultures.

In many other cross-cultural studies the cases are not individuals but cultures.[9] A good example of this latter kind of cross-cultural study is provided by Barry, Child, and Bacon (1959). This study is concerned with the relationship between accumulation of food resources and child-training. The authors define food accumulation as "the degree to which the food resources . . . are characteristically present in advance to be cared for or stored prior to being used, as against being consumed as soon as procured" (1959:53). They view the degree of food accumulation in a culture as a function of the type of subsistence economy it features. Cultures where subsistence is based on animal husbandry are assumed to be high in food accumulation since, in such cultures, "the meat that will be eaten in coming months and years, and the animals that will produce the future milk, are present on the hoof" (1959:52). Agricultural cultures are assumed to be moderately high on food accumulation since the harvest must be stored for future consumption. Cultures where the subsistence economy is based on hunting or fishing and that possess no means for preserving the catch are assumed to have a low degree of food accumulation.

Barry and his coauthors reason that in high-food-accumulation cultures, adults would tend to conform strongly to traditional routines designed to preserve the food supply and that innovation regarding economic activities would be discouraged. This would occur in such cultures, they argue, because ". . . carelessness in performance of routine duties leads to a threat of hunger, not for the day of carelessness itself but for many months to come" (1959:52).

In low-food-accumulation cultures, conversely, there is less likelihood of this danger arising from venturesomeness and initiative. If a hunter or fisherman tries a new approach, he may, if it fails, lose his day's catch. He can, however, immediately revert to traditional techniques in order to get the next day's catch. On the other hand, if the innovation is successful and produces a better catch than the traditional techniques, the hunter or fisherman is immediately benefited. Such cultures should, therefore, place a premium on innovativeness and assertion.

[9] It should also be noted in conjunction with our discussion of cross-cultural studies which treat entire cultures as cases, that determining what constitutes a single "culture" can prove highly problematic. A detailed discussion of the problem of identifying basic culture units (which is part of the so-called Galton-Flower's problem) is beyond the scope of this work. The interested reader is referred to the specialized treatments in Rohner (n.d.) and Naroll and Cohen (1970).

On this basis, Barry and his colleagues developed the hypothesis that high-food-accumulation cultures will feature child-training practices which emphasize compliance, while low-food-accumulation cultures will emphasize assertiveness in their child training. Following our usual format, we may state the hypothesis as follows:

INDEPENDENT VARIABLE	NATURE OF RELATIONSHIP	DEPENDENT VARIABLE
Accumulation of food	increases	stress on compliance as opposed to assertiveness in child-rearing practices.

In order to test this hypothesis, cultures that had subsistence economies based on animal husbandry or on agriculture combined with a substantial amount of animal husbandry were classed as "extremely high" in food accumulation. Hunting and fishing cultures were classed as "extremely low" in food accumulation. Measurement of the dependent variable involved a systematic assessment, made by two independent raters, of the relative preponderance of compliance or assertion in child-training practices. The raters did not know of the hypothesis to be tested at the time they assessed the ethnographic literature, although the degree of inter-rater reliability is, unfortunately, not reported. On the basis of these ratings, each culture in the sample was given a score on the dependent variable of compliance versus assertion. The scores ranged from —15 to +13.5. A high positive score indicates a high degree of compliance, while a high negative value indicates a high degree of assertiveness.

We can diagram Barry, Child, and Bacon's study as follows:

Treatment group (cultures with subsistence economies based on animal husbandry or agriculture with a substantial amount of animal husbandy)

$$\xleftarrow{\quad\quad ? \quad\quad}\rightarrow$$

[X   O]

Comparison group (cultures with subsistence economies based on hunting and fishing)

O

The question-marked double-headed arrow and the brackets around the X and O for the treatment group are used here to indicate that, *strictly speaking, we are only assuming the independent variable preceded the dependent variable.* Due to the lack of historical information, we cannot know for certain that a change in a system of high food accumulation occurred first and was followed by stress on compliance in child training in the various cultures that make up the treatment group. It is conceivable the sequence was actually the reverse. Thus, it might be argued that child training which stressed compliance developed first and caused the affected cultures to acquire subsistence economies that feature a high degree of food accumulation. This latter sequence, while conceivable, is sufficiently implausible that no one, to our knowledge, has seriously proposed it.

The results of the static group comparison showed, as predicted in the hypothesis, that the cultures in the treatment group, the group of cultures high in food accumulation, evidenced a much higher emphasis on compliance in their child training. This is graphically illustrated by Table 3.7 (p. 52). The number following each culture is its rating on the scale of compliance versus assertiveness. As may be ascertained from the table, the average score for the treatment group was 5.25 while that for the comparison group was —4.82. Statistical analysis indicated that the rival hypothesis of chance could be rejected since there was less than one chance out of a thousand that a difference this great would occur by chance alone.

It is sometimes argued that studies such as Barry, Child, and Bacon's, which use individual cultures as cases, largely avoid the problem of extraneous variables since these variables are "randomized out." Those who take this position would hold that since both the treatment and comparison groups are composed of many different cultures, it is difficult to conceive of any extraneous variables affecting one group of cultures substantially more than the other. Since both groups can be expected to be affected in roughly similar fashion by extraneous factors, so the argument goes, the possibility of error due to extraneous variables is remote.

There may be a grain of truth in this argument. The probability of error due to extraneous factors is no doubt somewhat less in such a study than in one like LeVine's, where the treatment and comparison groups may be expected to differ systematically on a great number of variables because all the cases in a given group are drawn from one culture. However, it must not be assumed that the problem of extraneous variables is totally eliminated when numerous cultures are used to supply the cases for a given group. It is still possible for treatment and comparison groups to be differentially affected by extraneous variables even though each group is composed of many different cultures. Thus, in the present example, Barry and his coauthors provide evidence that the cultures in the treatment group, in addition to being higher in food accumulation relative to the comparison group, also tend to be higher on variables such as degree of political integration, complexity of social stratification, and size of settlements. It is likely that the treatment and comparison groups differ on other extraneous variables as well—such as settlement density. Plausible rival hypotheses involving such extraneous factors might be offered as alternatives to the food-accumulation hypothesis. For example, such a hypothesis might be: In societies that have a high degree of settlement density, children will be trained to be nonassertive in order to minimize fighting between children of different families, which might lead to dangerous adult conflict.[10]

In evaluating this study according to our general criteria, we may note the following points. The paradigm employed appears to be the strongest possible under

[10] The researcher may, of course, attempt to deal with such rival hypotheses deriving from extraneous factors by control through matching or control through testing. While Barry et al. have not, strictly speaking, used either of these techniques, they have attempted, through statistical analysis, to demonstrate that rival hypotheses involving a number of extraneous factors are implausible (cf. Barry et al. 1959:59 f.).

TABLE 3.7   RELATION OF SUBSISTENCE ECONOMY TO GENERAL PRESSURE TOWARD
COMPLIANCE VERSUS ASSERTION IN CHILD-TRAINING[a]

	Extremely high accumulation cultures	Extremely low accumulation cultures
	Aymara (+13½)	
	Tepoztlan (+13½)	
	Lepcha (+11½)	
	Swazi (+ 8½)	
	Tswana (+ 8½)	
	Nyakyusa (+ 8)	
	Sotho (+ 8)	
	Nuer (+ 7)	
	Tallensi (+ 7)	
	Lovedu (+ 6½)	
	Mbundu (+ 6½)	
	Venda (+ 6½)	
	Kikuyu (+ 6)	
	Zulu (+ 6)	
	Pondo (+ 4½)	
	Chagga (+ 4)	
	Ganda (+ 3)	
	Chamorro (+ 2½)	Teton (+ 4)
	Masai (+ 2½)	Yahgan (+ 1)
	Chukchee (+ 1)	Hupa (+ ½)
Median[b]		
	Tanala (0)	Chiricahua (0)
	Thonga (− 2½)	Murngin (0)
	Araucanian (− 3)	Paiute (0)
	Balinese (− 3)	Arapaho (− 2)
		Kwakiutl (− 2)
		Cheyenne (− 2½)
		Kaska (− 2½)
		Klamath (− 2½)
		Ojibwa (− 2½)
		Ona (− 3)
		Aleut (− 4)
		Jicarilla (− 6½)
		Western Apache (−10)
		Siriono (−10½)
		West Greenland Eskimo (−11)
		Aranda (−12)
		Comanche (−12)
		Crow (−13½)
		Manus (−15)

[a] The cultures are "listed within each column in descending order of degree of pressure toward compliance as compared with pressure toward assertion. The number in parentheses after each society indicates the degree of preponderance of compliance (plus scores) or of assertion (minus scores)" (Barry et al. 1959:60).

[b] The dashed line marks the median point. When a set of scores is arranged in order according to the value of each score, the point that divides the ordering into two equal groups (one half considered to be "high" scores and the other "low" scores) is known as the *median*.

Adapted from Barry et al. 1959:60, Table 2. Reproduced by permission of the American Anthropological Association from the *American Anthropologist*, 61(1), 1959.

the circumstances. The replicability of the study is generally good, since details of sampling and measurement procedures are supplied. However, the reliability of the measure of assertion–compliance in child-training was not reported, although inter-rater reliability, at least, could have been determined since two raters were used in the study. Similarly, no formal evidence for the validity of the measure is provided. Finally, the role of chance was taken into account by means of appropriate statistical procedures.

Correlational Analysis as a Variant of the
Static-Group-Comparison Paradigm: Achievement
Motivation and Rates of Economic Growth

An approach to hypothesis-testing commonly employed in anthropological re-search is correlational analysis. Correlational analysis, in the form in which it is most commonly applied, can be viewed as a variant of the static-group-comparison paradigm. The major difference is that in correlational analysis many levels of the independent variable are utilized instead of only two as in the standard static group comparison.

To exemplify this difference, let us consider research by McClelland (1961) on achievement motivation and economic development. McClelland proposed the hy-pothesis that the rate of economic development of a country would be influenced by the level of achievement motivation among its people. This hypothesis may be stated as follows:

INDEPENDENT VARIABLE	NATURE OF RELATIONSHIP	DEPENDENT VARIABLE
The higher the level of achievement moti-vation among the people of a country	the higher its	rate of growth.

Achievement motivation, as you will recall from our discussion of LeVine's re-search in Nigeria, has been defined by McClelland as the degree to which a person desires to succeed in terms of some objective standard of excellence.

McClelland was able to measure achievement motivation by analyzing themes in children's readers. Each country in the study was assigned a score on achievement motivation on the basis of the frequency of achievement themes and achievement imagery in its children's readers in 1925. (The assumption was that the frequency of achievement themes and related imagery in a country's schoolbooks was an index of the average level of achievement motivation of the people in that country.) He derived a measure of economic development from the increase in the amount of electricity used per capita in each country over the following twenty-five year period. (The assumption behind this measure was that the amount of electricity used per person was an indication of how much modern machinery was in use and therefore an indicator of the degree of economic development in that country.) McClelland's measurements for twenty-two countries are reproduced in Table 3.8.

TABLE 3.8   ACHIEVEMENT MOTIVATION AND ECONOMIC DEVELOPMENT[a]

	Country	Scores on the independent variable, achievement motivation level, 1925	Scores on the dependent variable, economic development, 1950
	Ireland	3.19	0.33
	Australia	2.81	1.13
	Canada	2.67	1.73
Cases above	Sweden	2.19	3.17
Median on	Great Britain	2.10	1.65
Achievement	Denmark	2.00	0.14
Motive	U.S.A.	1.90	1.86
	Argentina	1.86	—0.61
	Austria	1.57	—0.12
	New Zealand	1.48	1.86
	Uruguay	1.48	—0.62
Median			
	Germany	1.38	—0.79
	Norway	1.33	—0.03
	Hungary	1.29	—0.26
Cases below	Chile	1.29	—0.43
Median on	Finland	1.24	0.74
Achievement	Union of S. Africa	1.05	0.69
Motive	Belgium	1.00	—0.75
	France	0.81	—0.55
	Spain	0.81	—0.63
	Greece	0.38	—0.52
	Netherlands	0.29	—0.10

[a] Cases are arranged according to their achievement motivation scores.
Adapted from McClelland, 1961:90–91, Table 3.4. From *The Achieving Society* by D. McClelland © 1961 by Litton Educational Publishing, Inc. Reprinted by permission of Van Nostrand Reinhold Company.

Using McClelland's data it is possible to construct a standard static group comparison. We can distinguish a treatment group, defined as those countries scoring high (that is, above the median) on the independent variable of achievement motivation and a comparison group, defined as those countries scoring low (below the median) on this variable. When this is done, we have, in effect, a standard static group comparison:

Treatment group   X   O
(the 11 countries   (a high
   above the median   level of
   on achievement   achievement
   motivation)   motivation)

Comparison group   O
(the 11 countries
   below the median
   on achievement
   motivation)

If we calculate the average economic development scores for the two groups we find that, consistent with the hypothesis, the treatment group scores more than twice as high on economic development (2.11) as the comparison group (0.99).

Casting these data into the form of an ordinary static group comparison is not, however, the most effective form of analysis. When quantitative or rank-order measurement of the independent variable has been achieved, as in this case, collapsing the measurements into two categories—"high" and "low"—obviously discards a great deal of information. That is, we know some of the cases in the "high" group have much more of the independent variable than others, yet we ignore this information and treat all the "high" group cases as having the same amount of this variable. Correlational analysis makes it possible to test for the hypothesized relationship using *all* the available information.

As we noted, correlational analysis, as it is usually applied, can be viewed as a type of static group comparison that uses many levels of the independent variable instead of only two as in the standard static group comparison. When we say that the standard static group comparison uses only two levels of treatment, we refer to the fact that one group, the treatment group, is exposed to a *high* level of the independent variable and another group, the comparison group, is exposed to a *low* level of the independent variable. By contrast, in correlational analysis, we deal with many levels of the independent variable. These two approaches to hypothesis-testing can be compared in the diagrams on page 56.

In the diagram for the correlational approach each of the X's represents a different level of the independent variable. The actual number of levels in a particular correlational analysis will depend upon how many different scores there are for a particular independent variable. If there are ten different scores on the independent variable in a sample, the correlational analysis will have ten different levels. Two or more cases may, of course, have the same score on the independent variable, in which case they will fall at the same level.

Now let us apply correlational analysis to the present example of McClelland's research. Instead of dividing the cases into two groups to construct a standard static group comparison, as before, we will this time allow each case to retain its individual score on the independent variable (as McClelland did). Of the 22 countries in McClelland's sample, three pairs of countries (New Zealand-Uruguay, Hungary-Chile, France-Spain) are tied on the independent variable. Thus, only 19 levels of the independent variable (achievement motivation) are represented in this sample of countries.

McClelland's hypothesis predicts that the dependent variable, economic growth, will increase as the independent variable of achievement motivation increases. Therefore, when we apply the correlational approach to these data, we would expect that, if the hypothesis is correct, we will observe an increase in the dependent variable as we go from the lower levels of the independent variable to the higher levels. In other words, there should be a tendency for cases high on the independent variable to be high on the dependent variable and for cases low on the independent variable to be low on the dependent variable.

We can form some idea of whether such a tendency exists by visually examining

STANDARD STATIC GROUP COMPARISON (Uses only two levels of the independent variable, "high" and "low.")		CORRELATIONAL APPROACH (Uses many levels of the independent variable. Here each level is represented by a separate subscripted X.)	
		$X_{\text{level } n}$	O
Treatment Group (exposed to a *high* level of the independent variable)	X O	. . .	
		$X_{\text{level } 6}$	O
		$X_{\text{level } 5}$	O
Comparison Group (exposed to a *low* level of the independent variable)	O	$X_{\text{level } 4}$	O
		$X_{\text{level } 3}$	O
		$X_{\text{level } 2}$	O
		$X_{\text{level } 1}$	O

a table of scores. Examination of Table 3.9 shows that there does appear to be a tendency for countries high on achievement motivation to be high on economic development and vice versa, although there are some nonconforming cases—for example, Argentina. As you can see, it is difficult to judge the strength of such a tendency by visual inspection alone. What is needed is some concise index of the strength of the tendency for two variables to vary together—that is, an index of the degree to which they are correlated (*co*-related). Mathematical procedures have been developed as an aid to correlational analysis and provide several indices of the strength of the relationship between two variables. These indices are known as correlation coefficients. One of the most widely used[11] correlation coefficients is Pearson's *r*. Pearson's *r* may range in value from -1.0 to $+1.0$. An *r* that approaches $+1.0$ indicates a very strong tendency for one variable to *increase* as the other increases; a value near 0.0 indicates there is almost no tendency for one variable to increase as the other increases; and a value near -1.0 indicates a very strong tendency for one variable to *decrease* as the other increases.

When a Pearson's *r* correlation coefficient is computed for the McClelland data it yields a value of .54, indicating a moderately strong tendency for the dependent variable to increase as the independent variable increases. However, in correlational analysis, as in other research, we must be alert to the role of chance. It is possible for chance alone to produce the appearance of some correlation between dependent and independent variables in a sample of cases when in fact no rela-

[11] Pearson's *r* has won such wide acceptance as a measure of correlation that in the social science literature, whenever reference is made to the "correlation coefficient" this is understood as a reference to Pearson's *r*. Other measures of correlation have been developed, however.

TABLE 3.9   ACHIEVEMENT MOTIVATION AND ECONOMIC DEVELOPMENT[a]

Level of independent variable	Country	Scores on the independent variable, achievement motivation level, 1925	Scores on the dependent variable, economic development, 1950
Level 19	Ireland	3.19	0.33
Level 18	Australia	2.81	1.13
Level 17	Canada	2.67	1.73
Level 16	Sweden	2.19	3.17
Level 15	Great Britain	2.10	1.65
Level 14	Denmark	2.00	0.14
Level 13	United States	1.90	1.86
Level 12	Argentina	1.86	—0.61
Level 11	Austria	1.57	—0.12
Level 10	New Zealand	1.48	1.86
	Uruguay	1.48	—0.62
Level 9	Germany	1.38	—0.79
Level 8	Norway	1.33	—0.03
Level 7	Hungary	1.29	—0.26
	Chile	1.29	—0.43
Level 6	Finland	1.24	0.74
Level 5	Union of S. Africa	1.05	0.69
Level 4	Belgium	1.00	—0.75
Level 3	France	0.81	—0.55
	Spain	0.81	—0.63
Level 2	Greece	0.38	—0.52
Level 1	Netherlands	0.29	—0.10

[a] Cases are arranged according to their achievement motive scores and the different levels of the independent variable are distinguished.
Adapted from McClelland, 1961:90–91, Table 3.4. From *The Achieving Society* by D. McClelland © 1961 by Litton Educational Publishing, Inc. Reprinted by permission of Van Nostrand Reinhold Company.

tionship exists. Statistical procedures have been developed to estimate the role of chance in correlational analysis (Hardyck and Petrinovich 1969:203 f.). By applying these we find that so strong a correlation between the two variables in the McClelland study would be obtained by chance alone less than one time out of a hundred. Therefore, we are probably safe in rejecting chance as a factor here.

Thus, this correlational analysis, which makes full use of the information contained in the data, supports the hypothesis that a high level of achievement motivation produces a high rate of economic growth. However, the support for this hypothesis, like that found for any other, is subject to the limitations of the structure of the research. Let us consider, therefore, the types of error to which a correlational analysis of the type discussed here is particularly vulnerable.

Although a correlational analysis may be viewed as a variant of the static group comparison, two kinds of error that plague the standard version of this paradigm —selection and interaction effects involving selection—do not apply to correlational analysis since there are no treatment and comparison groups. All the cases in the typical correlational analysis are considered collectively. However, correlational analysis is *highly subject to errors resulting from extraneous variables.* It is this potential source of error that lies behind the oft-repeated refrain, "correlation doesn't prove causation." That is, a high correlation between an independent and dependent variable may be entirely due to the effect of some extraneous variable that varies together with the independent variable. We might, for example, encounter a situation in which the independent variable has no effect on the dependent variable, but both the independent and dependent variables are affected by a third extraneous variable:

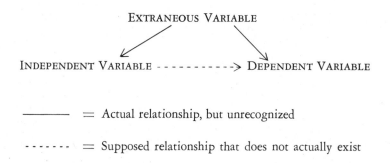

————— = Actual relationship, but unrecognized

- - - - - - = Supposed relationship that does not actually exist

This would produce a high correlation between the independent and dependent variables since they are simultaneously and similarly influenced by the extraneous variable. Because of this, a researcher would be in danger of mistakenly concluding that the independent variable affects the dependent variable. An example of such a situation would be a high correlation between champagne consumption and teachers' salaries. That is, it might be that in cities where champagne consumption is high, teachers' salaries also tend to be high, and vice versa. A rash investigator might be tempted to view champagne consumption as an independent variable affecting teachers' salaries, on the grounds that school board members, when happily inebriated, will tend to grant higher salaries to teachers:

CHAMPAGNE CONSUMPTION - - - - - - -> TEACHERS' SALARIES

However, such a correlation would almost certainly result from an extraneous factor of average income, which affects both champagne consumption and teachers' salaries:

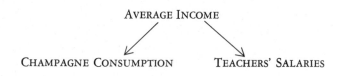

This kind of error in correlational analysis is analogous to the error that may arise in a standard static group comparison when the treatment and comparison groups are differentially affected by extraneous variables (when there is selection–extraneous-variable interaction).

The effects of particular extraneous variables in a correlation analysis may be eliminated by a special procedure known as partial correlation. In this technique, the effects of the extraneous variable are removed mathematically. This technique thus fills somewhat the same role in correlational analysis as does matching in the standard static group comparison, making it possible, in effect, to control specific extraneous variables.

A further difficulty often encountered in correlational analysis is uncertainty concerning the direction of influence. In McClelland's study this was *not* a problem, as achievement motivation was measured in 1925, while rate of economic development was measured over the period 1925–1950. *If* there is a causal relationship between the two variables, then clearly the temporally earlier variable of achievement motivation must be causing the temporally later variable of economic development. It could hardly be maintained that subsequent economic development caused the level of achievement motivation in 1925. Often, however, the time sequence of the variables in a correlational analysis is not known and can only be assumed. This, of course, introduces further uncertainty into the analysis. This problem, it should be pointed out, is not unique to correlational analysis. Indeed, one of our examples of the standard static group comparison, the Barry, Child, and Bacon study, featured this type of uncertainty concerning the temporal sequence of events.

In evaluating McClelland's research according to our general evaluative criteria, we can make the following observations. The paradigm employed, the correlational variant of the static group comparison, appears to be the strongest possible given the nature of the research problem. Since it makes full use of the detailed information available on the independent variable, it is notably superior to the standard static group comparison. It is also important to note, however, that in the test of this particular hypothesis, McClelland was able to guard against only a few of the potential extraneous variables (such as the effect of World War II damage on some countries in his sample) and his findings are weakened by this.[12]

The measure of achievement motivation, the independent variable, appears to possess satisfactory reliability. The reliability of this measure was assessed in two ways. First, interrater reliability was computed. The measure involves, as we noted, scoring stories from children's readers for indications of a concern with achievement. As two judges working independently were used to score the stories, it was

---

[12] In fairness, however, it must also be pointed out that this hypothesis is only one of a complex array of hypotheses concerning achievement motivation that McClelland has tested. Taken together, these hypotheses make it difficult to identify particular extraneous variables that could be producing the correlations he has found. We will discuss the importance of this strategy of multiple hypothesis-testing, or the strategy of "cumulative, complementary research" in more detail later (page 105). For a recent, outstanding example of such cumulative, complementary research by anthropologists, see Cole et al. (1971).

possible to compute interrater reliability, which was found to be quite high. Second, split-half reliability was determined. The twenty-one stories for each country were divided into sets of ten and eleven stories apiece and the scores for one set were correlated with the scores on the other set. This operation revealed an acceptably high split-half reliability.

The measure of economic development, the dependent variable, also seems likely to possess a satisfactory level of reliability, since procedures for measuring electricity consumption are highly developed technically and are well standardized throughout the world.

As regards validity, the measure of achievement motivation used is a direct extension of another measure that has been shown rather convincingly to be valid (see McClelland et al. 1953). Thus, it might reasonably be maintained that the modified measure used in this study is also likely to be valid. More direct evidence of its validity is, of course, to be desired. The measure of economic development, derived from electricity consumption per capita, possesses a great deal of face validity, since electricity consumption is intimately connected with modern economic growth. The validity of this measure is further supported by the fact that it correlates quite highly with a measure of per capita real income, Colin Clark's "international unit" income measure (McClelland 1961:80–87).

The replicability of the study appears to be satisfactory. Detailed descriptions are provided for all major procedures utilized. The steps taken to deal with the rival hypothesis of chance also appear satisfactory. As we noted, a statistical test indicated that there was only a very small possibility that the results of the study were due to chance.

In concluding this review of McClelland's study, one final comment seems appropriate. It is apparent that McClelland's hypothesis does not fully account for the variation in the measure of economic growth for the sample countries, since the data show only a moderately strong relationship between the independent variable of achievement motivation and economic growth. This suggests that other factors besides achievement motivation also contribute to economic development. Many of the phenomena studied by anthropologists have multiple causes and it is therefore exceedingly rare for a simple one-factor hypothesis such as the one reviewed here to account completely for the variation in the dependent variable. Of course, it would be naive in the extreme to reject a hypothesis because it only accounted for a part of the variation in the dependent variable. What is called for is the elaboration of the hypothesis to incorporate other important independent variables as well.

THE PRETEST–POSTTEST PARADIGM

Social Contact and Attitude Change

An example of the pretest–posttest paradigm is provided by the research of Festinger and Kelley (1951). The setting for this research was a large government-financed housing project in a small eastern American city. A research team that did a preliminary survey of the project found a low degree of social contact, with few residents enjoying active friendships within the project. Project residents, in fact, expressed a high degree of hostility toward one another, viewing their project neighbors as "low class" and "undesirable." The researchers found that project residents, as a group, were actually no lower in status than other people in the community, according to objective indicators such as education and occupation. They ascertained, however, that, originally, most project residents had not wanted to move into the project and saw themselves as having been forced to move there by various circumstances beyond their control, such as a shortage of housing. The researchers speculated that the residents' generally unfavorable initial expectations about the project had prevented them from forming many social contacts after moving into it. This lack of contact among project dwellers then perpetuated their unfavorable attitudes toward one another. Their analysis of the situation led the researchers to form the hypothesis that "an action program which stimulated contact among project residents under favorable conditions would act to break down their hostile attitudes toward each other," or, in diagrammatic form:

INDEPENDENT VARIABLE	NATURE OF RELATIONSHIP	DEPENDENT VARIABLE
Contact under favorable conditions	decreases	hostile attitudes.

To test this hypothesis, Festinger and Kelley utilized a pretest–posttest paradigm. Professional community workers set up a series of community activity programs in the project, including a nursery school program and various recreational activities programs for school age children, teen-agers, and adults. The overall program of community activities began with a two and one-half month period in which the community workers explained the various activity programs to the project residents and attempted to interest them in taking part. At the end of this introductory phase, an attitude survey was carried out among a sample of project residents. Unfavorable attitudes toward other members of the project were measured by ascertaining whether persons interviewed made "hostile" comments (as judged by the researchers on the basis of responses to a standard list of interview questions) regarding other project residents. Then followed a second period of two and one-half months during which residents became actively involved in the various community programs. At the conclusion of this second period the attitude survey was repeated using another sample of project residents. The activity program then was continued for still another two and one-half month period, after which the attitude survey was administered for the third and last time.

The timing of the study is summarized in Figure 3.1.

FIGURE 3.1

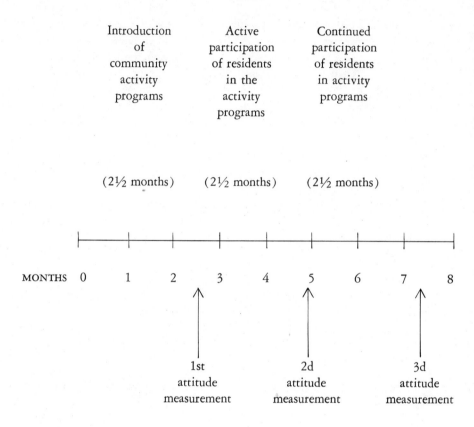

You will note that *three* measurements were carried out instead of the two that are standard for the pretest–posttest paradigm. We may view Festinger and Kelley's study as constituting two sequential pretest–posttest studies, with the middle measurement constituting the posttest for the first study and the pretest for the second. This may be diagrammed as follows:

a) First pretest–posttest study

    O   X   O

(first attitude   (exposure to 2½   (second
  measurement)   month period   attitude
                 during which   measure-
                 residents   ment)
                 became actively
                 involved in
                 community
                 activity programs)

b) Second pretest–posttest study

O	X	O
(second attitude measurement)	(exposure to second 2½ month period during which residents continued participation in community activity programs)	(third attitude measurement)

The results of the two pretest–posttest studies are shown in Table 3.10.

To sum up these results, the total percentage of "hostile" comments increased slightly during the first study (that is, between the first and second surveys), and increased somewhat more during the second study (between the second and third surveys). These results obviously do not support the hypothesis. If anything, they suggest that the community activities may have *increased* negative attitudes among the residents. The explanation for the failure of the hypothesis, however, does not lie in failure of the community activities programs to actually stimulate increased contact among residents. Overall, the amount of social contact was substantially increased. Survey data showed that the average number of different project residents who were invited into the respondents' homes increased from 3.7, at the time of the first survey, to 5.5 and 6.4, for the second and third surveys. The research results, then, cast doubt on the validity of the hypothesis that increased contact, per se, will reduce negative attitudes. Rather, it may be, as the authors suggest, that, "What impact these contacts have on attitudes . . . depends on the nature of the contact rather than its mere occurrence" (1951:71).

It would seem that the pretest–posttest paradigm was probably the strongest paradigm feasible in this situation, as there apparently were no other projects in the area which could have provided a comparison group. (Had such a comparison group been available, the study might have utilized the more powerful nonequivalent control group paradigm.) Since the pretest–posttest paradigm is employed,

TABLE 3.10   PERCENTAGES OF "HOSTILE" ATTITUDES ON THE THREE MEASUREMENT OCCASIONS

Attitude measurement occasion	Percentage expressing attitude that "Neighbors are low class"	Percentage expressing attitude that "Neighbors are not cooperative"
1st	21	34
2d	22	35
3d	32	38

[a] Adapted from Festinger and Kelley 1951:70. Used by permission of Research Center for Group Dynamics, Institute for Social Research, University of Michigan.

extraneous variables pose a substantial problem in this study, as in most studies where this paradigm is used. Any extraneous variable that changed over the same time period as the independent variable (increased contact) must be suspected of influencing the dependent variable (in this case, negative attitudes). The problem, of course, grows more serious as the length of time between the measurements increases. Since the time between measurements was approximately two and one-half months for both pretest–posttest studies involved in this research, a consider-able number of extraneous variables could have changed during these intervals. It is easy to envision extraneous variables that might have influenced the outcome—for example, if there had been a substantial increase in burglary or other crime in the project during the critical periods, this might have increased the residents' negative attitudes.

The problem of extraneous variables may be lessened by careful monitoring of events that occur during the interval between measurements. If, as in this case, the researchers are able to continuously observe the research situation, it is likely that major changes in extraneous variables such as crime rate will be noticed. If the researcher has reason to expect that one or several particular extraneous variables may prove troublesome, he can control for this source of error by arranging to measure these variables. If he can show by these measurements that the suspect extraneous variables have not, in fact, changed during the period of the research, he can rule them out as rival hypotheses. If control through measurement of ex-traneous variables is not possible, the researcher should at least try to keep a careful log of occurrences during the interval between measurements, so as to maximize the chances that he will be aware of any changes in extraneous variables which might provide rival hypotheses to the one he is testing.

As noted in Chapter 2, the pretest–posttest paradigm also is subject to error from reactive measurement effects. You will recall that we have defined reactive measure-ment error as change in the dependent variable due solely to the measurement process itself. Although the questions in the structured interview used to assess hostile attitudes were carefully phrased in a neutral manner, there is at least a possibility that the interview itself might have acted subtly to change people's views about their fellow project residents. The researchers in this study, however, employed a method of sampling which reduced the possibility of error due to reactive measurements. Instead of interviewing exactly the same sample of project residents in the three surveys, they selected a new random sample of residents for each survey, with the result that the majority of those interviewed in the second and third surveys had not been interviewed before. This procedure should have considerably reduced any effects from reactive measurements.[13]

We can make the following observations regarding the reliability and validity of the measure of hostile attitudes, the dependent variable. The scoring of inter-view responses for "hostile expression" was done, we are told, in accordance with a content analysis scheme developed specifically for this study. No details of the coding scheme are given, however, and no information on interrater reliability is

---

[13] It is possible to guard completely against reactive measurement effects in a pretest–posttest paradigm by taking measurements from two entirely separate random samples of informants—that is, by insuring that none of the persons included in the pretest random sample are included in the posttest random sample (cf. Campbell and Stanley 1966:53–54).

provided. Festinger and Kelley do comment that, "to insure a continuing high level of agreement between coders, periodic group discussions of specific problems in the code and constant supervision and check coding were instituted" (1951:80). It would appear from this that a satisfactory level of interrater reliability was achieved, but specific information on the degree of this reliability is needed. Similarly, no formal evidence for the validity of the content analysis measure of hostile attitudes is provided. It might reasonably be argued, however, that this method possesses considerable face validity. Certainly, responding to the rather bland interview questions used—for example, "What things about the project make it easy or hard to have community activities?"—with expressions of hostility toward one's fellow project residents would seem, on the face of it, to indicate a certain degree of hostility.

The replicability of the study would have been considerably enhanced if we had been supplied with details of the procedures used in the content analysis of the interviews, and of the various community activity programs. Lacking this information, it would be difficult to replicate the study. Comprehensive information was provided, however, on other important aspects of the study, including sampling techniques and the interview used.

THE NONEQUIVALENT-CONTROL-GROUP PARADIGM

Achievement Training in India

We have already discussed two studies dealing with achievement motivation. One, McClelland's 1961 study, suggested that the level of achievement motivation in a society is an important variable for the study of economic development, since the average level of achievement motivation in a society appears to partly determine its rate of economic growth. The second study, by LeVine, hypothesized that one of the determinants of the level of achievement motivation in a society is the nature of its "status mobility system." Recently, a great deal of attention has been paid to other possible determinants of achievement motivation. Researchers have, in particular, begun to explore the question of whether it might be possible for a person to increase deliberately his own personal level of achievement motivation. If a practical means of doing so is found, it might become possible for large numbers of persons in a society to voluntarily raise their level of achievement motivation, resulting, perhaps, in their society's (as well as, possibly, their own) rate of economic development being accelerated.

Accordingly, McClelland and Winter (1969) developed the hypothesis that achievement motivation might be increased by a specific course of instruction which included the following types of training inputs:

Teaching participants how to recognize and create achievement-oriented fantasy;
Encouraging them to consider how achievement relates to their own life-situations;
Guiding them in setting specific achievement goals and establishing guidelines by which their success may be judged;
Providing interpersonal supports for changes in motives.[14]

[14] A full description of the components of the course may be found in McClelland and Winter (1969:45–78).

In order to test their hypothesis, McClelland and Winter designed a study that employed the nonequivalent-control-group paradigm. They arranged to make the course they had designed available at a research institute in India. They then contacted a number of businessmen from several Indian cities and after fully explaining the aims of the course, invited them to participate. A number of these men volunteered for the course and went ahead to complete it. These men constituted the treatment group. To obtain a comparison group, they contacted other businessmen who resembled the volunteers in important characteristics and were from the same cities.

A number of different measures of the dependent variable of achievement motivation were constructed. The basic measure used, the one which will be reported here, was a Business Activity Level scale developed for the study. Since all the participants were businessmen, it was expected that any increases in achievement motivation would be reflected in an increase in their business activity. The researchers therefore developed a set of criteria by which a man's business activity level could be scored. The scale ranged from -1, indicating a low level of activity in business, to $+2$, indicating the man was highly active. Interviews were conducted with the members of the treatment and comparison groups about two years after the conclusion of the course and information was collected on the personal and business activities of each. On the basis of this information, the business activity level of each of the men was scored for the two years prior to the time of the course (the years 1962–1964) and the two years following (1964–1966). (It should be emphasized that these measures of business activity were *reconstructed* from later information provided by informants.)

The McClelland and Winter study may be diagrammed as follows:

Treatment
Group   O   X   O
              (reconstructed   (exposure to the   (reconstructed
               premeasurement   achievement   postmeasurement
               of business   motivation   of business
               activity)   training course)   activity)

Comparison
Group   O   O
              (reconstructed   (reconstructed
               premeasurement   postmeasurement
               of business   of business
               activity)   activity)

The results of the study, in terms of business activity levels, are presented in Table 3.11. The treatment group, as predicted by the hypothesis, showed a marked increase in the percentage of persons who could be classified as active ($+2$) on the business activity scale. The comparison group showed only a very slight increase. A test of statistical significance indicated that it was very unlikely that these

TABLE 3.11 PERCENTAGE OF TREATMENT AND COMPARISON GROUP SUBJECTS CLASSIFIED AS ACTIVE (SCORING $+2$ ON THE BUSINESS ACTIVITY SCALE) DURING TWO YEAR PERIODS

	Before course 1962–1964 (percent)	After course 1964–1966 (percent)	Net percentage increase
Treatment Group	18	51	33
Comparison Group	22	25	3

Adapted from McClelland and Winter 1969:213, Table 7.2. Copyright © 1969 the authors. Used by permission.

differences were due to chance, since the probability of obtaining such great differences through chance alone was less than one in a thousand.

The use of the nonequivalent-control-group paradigm in this study means that this research is relatively invulnerable to one source of error that would plague the weaker static-group-comparison paradigm used in a similar situation. This is the rival hypothesis that the difference between the groups simply reflects pre-existing differences in the business activity levels of the comparison and treatment groups because of the manner in which the members of the group were selected. Thus, had a simple static group comparison been employed it might be maintained that the selection process—namely, using volunteers for the treatment group, while the comparison group was composed of nonvolunteers—had caused men with higher levels of business activity to be included in the treatment group. This would assume that more active businessmen will be more likely to volunteer for such a course. If, because of selection, the men in the treatment group were more active to begin with—that is, prior to their exposure to the independent variable—a static group comparison would show the two groups to be different even if the men simply maintained their original activity scores and the independent variable had no effect. A nonequivalent-control-group paradigm, such as the one used here, can distinguish between preexisting differences due to selection and differences which develop following exposure to the independent variable since it is the gain scores (the differences between the premeasurements and postmeasurements) that are compared and not the postmeasurement differences. Therefore, in this research we can reject the rival hypothesis of preexisting differences due to selection.

The only danger from selection when a nonequivalent-control-group paradigm is used is the possibility of interaction effects involving selection. Thus, it is conceivable that the volunteers who make up the treatment group in this study differed from the nonvolunteers in being more open to the exploitation of new business opportunities. If important new business opportunities developed during the study, the treatment group members might have taken greater advantage of them thereby increasing their level of business activity relative to the comparison group members. Such an interaction between selection and the extraneous factor of new business opportunities could cause the treatment group to show a significant gain relative to the comparison group, even if the independent variable had no effect. We cannot reject this particular rival hypothesis in the present study, and it may be possible to develop other rival hypotheses involving selection interactions as well.

The possibility of interaction effects involving selection would have been greatly reduced, if not totally eliminated, if McClelland and Winter had found it possible to draw the members of the comparison group from among those who volunteered to take the course—that is, if they had randomly assigned volunteers to take the course or not take it. Had this been done, the study would have employed the control-group paradigm, which is stronger than the nonequivalent-control-group design precisely because it is resistant to selection interaction effects.

A major question concerning the McClelland and Winter study pertains to the validity of their measure of business activity. It will be recalled that all the data on a subject's business activity were collected from the subject himself roughly two years after he had completed the course. Measurements of this sort are subject to systematic distortion that may itself constitute a rival hypotheses to the one being tested. It might be, for example, that those who went through the course of training feel some need to demonstrate that it has been effective. Thus, as McClelland and Winter themselves note (1969:208–209), informants may tend consciously or unconsciously to distort their recollection of past business experiences in order to give the impression of improvement. Such distortion could create the appearance that the independent variable had had an effect when it in fact had none. Alternatively, some of the individuals in the comparison group who knew of the training program might have felt a need to demonstrate that they had made just as much progress as those in the treatment group and, as a result, might have consciously or unconsciously enhanced their recent business activity. Such distortion could obscure a real effect on the part of the independent variable. This source of error could have been reduced or eliminated by using measurements that were not so subject to memory error and intentional distortion. For example, as a substitute, the researchers might have interviewed the associates of the participants in the study both before the independent variable was introduced and afterwards, to ascertain the participants' levels of business activity. If this had been done there might have been less possibility of memory error and/or intentional distortion.

In sum, the validity of the measurements in this study is compromised by the dependence on reconstructed measures. Moreover, the interrater reliability for the rating system used to assign business activity scores is not reported, although an earlier version of the scoring system was said to have exhibited the relatively high interrater reliability of .92.

The replicability of the study is generally good, as the authors are careful to supply details of the various procedures employed. The study also incorporates provisions for dealing with the role of chance, since, as mentioned above, an appropriate statistical test was employed.

Innovation Adoption in Puerto Rico

An interesting anthropological study using the nonequivalent-control-group paradigm was carried out by Suchman, Cebollero, Munoz, and Pabon (1967). Their study dealt with the acceptance of an innovation, a topic currently receiving considerable attention in applied anthropology. The innovation in question was a newly developed glove designed to protect cane-cutters' hands from injury due to misdirected machete blows, and from sores and skin irritation due to contact with cane stalks. In Puerto Rico, where the study was done, such injuries have constituted a major and continuing problem for cane-cutters.

One hypothesis to be tested by the study was that acceptance of an innovation, such as the protective glove, could be effectively promoted by bringing community pressure to bear on the intended recipients, in this case the cane-cutters. The idea was to enlist the support of community leaders in a campaign to promote the innovation. This, it was hypothesized, would induce the cane-cutters in the community to accept the glove. The rationale for this was that "since the individual shares the needs and attitudes of his sociocultural system, it is to be expected that if the group accepts an innovation, individual members will tend to accept it also" (Suchman et al. 1967:215).

This hypothesis may be paraphrased as follows:

INDEPENDENT VARIABLE	NATURE OF RELATIONSHIP	DEPENDENT VARIABLE
Support of community	will promote	adoption of an innovation.

To test this hypothesis, two "reasonably comparable" communities were selected for study. In one community, a strong effort was made to enlist the support of the community leaders for a campaign to promote the use of the protective glove. These leaders agreed to participate and several community meetings were held to discuss the campaign. A meeting was also held for the wives, mothers, and daughters of cane-cutters.

A second community provided a comparison group. Here no attempt was made to enlist the support of community leaders. Instead, the emphasis was placed on exposing the cane-cutters directly to educational material—including pamphlets and films—advocating use of the glove.

Subsequently, protective gloves were made available in both communities to workers who asked for them. Records were kept of how many workers accepted the glove and of how long those who accepted the gloves continued to use them.

This study, as was suggested above, can be viewed as employing the nonequivalent-control-group paradigm. This is true in spite of the fact that no premeasurements were obtained by Suchman et al. Our reason for classifying this study as using the nonequivalent-control-group paradigm is that it can legitimately be assumed, in this sort of situation, that prior measurements would have shown a zero level of the dependent variable (adoption of an innovation—in the present instance, a protective glove). Since, in this study, the innovation was unavailable to both groups until after the treatment group had been exposed to the independent variable, premeasurements, had they been made, would necessarily have shown no acceptance. The study may be diagrammed as follows:

Treatment Group (cane-cutters in the community where the community-pressure approach was used)	O (premeasurement of dependent variable of adoption of glove assumed to be zero)	X (enlisting support of community leaders for use of the glove)	O (whether or not worker accepted and continued to use glove)
Comparison Group (cane-cutters in the community where the direct educational approach was used)	O (premeasurement of dependent variable of adoption of glove assumed to be zero)		O (whether or not worker accepted and continued to use glove)

It was found that the rate of adoption of the glove (defined as accepting and continuing to use the glove for the duration of the study) was 19 percent in the treatment group, as compared to 76 percent in the comparison group. Obviously the community pressure hypothesis does not fare very well. The authors suggest that the following might have been among the factors involved in its failure. The community which provided the treatment group of cane-cutters was in a "state of flux" and the leadership structure was "diffuse and divided" (Suchman et al. 1967: 220). Under these conditions it is perhaps not surprising that community pressure was relatively ineffective in promoting acceptance of the innovation.

It should be stressed that if it could not safely be assumed that premeasurements would show a zero rate of adoption—which would have been the case, for example, if some protective gloves had been in use before the research began—this study would not represent an example of the nonequivalent-control-group paradigm. It would instead constitute an instance of the weaker static-group-comparison paradigm. Then the rival hypothesis of selection, which is ruled out by the nonequivalent-control-group paradigm, would have to be seriously considered.

The reliability and validity of the measure of the dependent variable in this study, adoption of the protective glove, would appear to be very high indeed, as the measure consists simply of observing whether or not the worker accepts and continues to use it. The replicability of the study is good as full details are provided of the procedures employed. No formal means were used to assess the role of chance, but it appears from examination of the results that a standard test of significance would show a very low probability of the results being due to chance.

CONTROL-GROUP PARADIGM

The control-group paradigm, since it requires random assignment of cases to treatment and comparison groups, is perhaps rarely feasible in the naturalistic research settings of interest to most anthropologists. However, studies by Lefkowitz,

Blake and Mouton (1955), Berelson and Freedman (1964), Freedman and Takeshita (1969), and Takeshita (1966) demonstrate how this powerful paradigm may sometimes be effectively applied under natural conditions.

Status, Models, and Violation of Prohibitions

Two hypotheses of interest to Lefkowitz and his coworkers in their 1955 study were: (a) people will be more likely to violate a prohibition when they have witnessed another person violating it; and (b) if the person who is seen to violate the prohibition (the "model") is of high status, he will be imitated more often than if he is of low status:

INDEPENDENT VARIABLE	NATURE OF RELATIONSHIP	DEPENDENT VARIABLE
a) Witnessing a violating model	increases	tendency to violate a prohibition.
b) Witnessing a violating model of high status (as opposed to one of low status)	will result in a greater increase in	tendency to violate a prohibition.

To test these hypotheses, the researchers focused on a natural setting, three street corners in Austin, Texas. This setting contained prohibitions in the form of traffic signal lights that alternately signaled pedestrians to "wait" or "walk." Two "models" were employed by the researchers. One was dressed in a manner which, in that area and at that time, implied high status—he wore "a freshly pressed suit, shined shoes, white shirt, tie, and straw hat." The second model was dressed in a manner to imply low status—"well-worn scuffed shoes, soiled patched trousers and an unpressed blue denim shirt." Actually, both models were portrayed by the same person, a man in his early thirties who made the transition from one model to another simply by changing his clothes.

The procedure used was for either the high- or the low-status model to cross the intersection during the middle of the "wait" signal. Pedestrians who happened to be standing with the model before he crossed the street were then observed from a distance to see whether they imitated the model in disobeying the prohibition. A number of trials were made at the various street corners over a period of three days. Observations were also made during a comparable number of intervals during which no model was present in order to ascertain the frequency of violations in the absence of a model. The timing of the various trials was carefully arranged to avoid any consistent relationship between time of day and type of trial.

This study can be said to employ the postmeasurement-only version of the control-group paradigm (see p. 17, footnote 10), since it can reasonably be maintained that the appearance of individual pedestrians at a street corner during a particular interval of time is essentially a random process. Thus, the researchers took advantage of a kind of natural randomization process to achieve something close to random assignment of cases to treatment and comparison groups. This made it possible to assume that the two groups were equivalent prior to exposure of the treatment group to the independent variable.

The test of the first hypothesis, that people will be more likely to violate a prohibition when they have witnessed a model violating it, can be diagrammed in our usual manner, as follows:

Treatment Group (pedestrians witnessing a violating model)	R (natural random assignment of pedestrians)	X (witnessing models— both high and low status—violate the prohibition on crossing the street)	O (whether pedestrians violated the prohibition)
Comparison Group (pedestrians not witnessing a violating model)	R (natural random assignment of pedestrians)		O (whether pedestrians violated the prohibition)

The results for this first hypothesis are summarized in Table 3.12. The prediction that violations will increase with exposure to a violating model is strongly supported, there being an increase from 1 percent violations for the comparison group

TABLE 3.12   THE EFFECT OF THE PRESENCE OF A MODEL ON PEDESTRIAN VIOLATIONS

	Pedestrians obeying prohibition	Pedestrians violating prohibition	Percentage of violators
Exposed to Violating Model (includes both high and low status models)	526	52	9
Not Exposed to Violating Model	742	8	1

Adapted from Lefkowitz et al. 1955:705, Table 1. Copyright 1955 by the American Psychological Assn. Used by permission.

to 9 percent for the treatment group. A statistical test showed that this difference was very unlikely to have been due to chance. The test of the second hypothesis can be diagrammed as follows:

Treatment
Group   R   X   O
(pedestrians   (natural random   (exposure   (whether
  witnessing   assignment of   to a high   pedestrians
  a high   pedestrians)   rather than   violate the
  status   low status   prohibition)
  model)   violating
                                             model)

Comparison
Group   R   O
(pedestrians   (natural random   (whether
  witnessing   assignment of   pedestrians
  a low   pedestrians)   violate the
  status   prohibition)
  model)

Table 3.13 presents the data relevant to this hypothesis. The second prediction from this hypothesis (that exposure to a high-status model will result in a greater tendency to violate a prohibition than will exposure to a low-status model) is also sustained. More than three times as many pedestrians violated the signal after observing a high-status violating model than did so after witnessing a low-status violating model. And again, as in the case of the first hypothesis, a standard statistical test showed that this difference was very unlikely to have been due to chance.

TABLE 3.13   THE EFFECT OF ROLE MODEL STATUS ON PEDESTRIAN VIOLATIONS

	Pedestrians obeying prohibition	Pedestrians violating prohibition	Percentage of pedestrians violating prohibition
Exposure to High-Status Violating Model	250	40	14
Exposure to Low-Status Violating Model	276	12	4

Adapted from Lefkowitz et al. 1955:705, Table 1. Copyright 1955 by the American Psychological Assn. Used by permission.

There is relatively little to criticize concerning this study. The paradigm used, the control-group paradigm is a very strong one. There is, perhaps, one point of uncertainty concerning the randomization process. It is only an assumption that the arrival of pedestrians at an intersection during a particular interval is essentially a random process. However, there seems to us little reason to question such an assumption.

The reliability of the measurements used seems likely to be high since the measurement process consisted simply of an observer's recording violations or non-violations by pedestrians. The measure also appears to be valid since it is actually a sample of the behavior which it is desired to measure—violation of a prohibition. The study is described in sufficient detail to provide for easy replication, and statistical tests were employed to ascertain that the differences obtained were unlikely to be due to chance alone.

Fertility Control in Taiwan

Population growth is a serious issue of great practical importance in all parts of the world today. Like the weather, however, it appears that more people are talking about it than are doing something effective about it. To be sure, many groups, agencies, foundations, and countries are working to alter the potentially disastrous trend toward rapid population growth. However, the question is, "How effective are these efforts?" Many programs can point to changes in birth rates or contraceptive-use rates, but it is not always clear that these differences are due to the program making the claim.

A recent study of a program to increase the percentage of Taiwanese women using contraceptive devices (and in this way to lower the birth rate) provides a useful illustration of how the control-group paradigm may be employed to test hypotheses concerning the efficacy of such programs of directed change. This study thus has particular relevance for applied anthropology. The following summary of this research is based on reports by Takeshita (1966), Berelson and Freedman (1964), and Freedman and Takeshita (1969).

Preparatory research was begun in 1962 *before* the start of the family-planning campaign. At the time, Taiwan's population was 12,256,682, distributed over 14,047 square miles of land (an average of 873 persons per square mile). Birth rates were declining slowly but death rates were declining rapidly. The result was a steady annual growth in population of 3 percent. The initial research indicated the vast majority (about 90 percent) of women in the prime reproductive ages of 20–39 wanted to limit the size of their families but did not know how to do so effectively. Generally, they were anxious to learn about more effective means for doing so, especially if they already had a few children, including at least one son. The goal of the campaign then became one of transforming existing attitudes into action rather than of convincing women that they should desire to have fewer children.

The campaign itself was begun after this prestudy had been completed, and the large city of Taichung was chosen as the site. The program was massive and complex. Berelson and Freedman suggest that it also constituted "one of the most extensive and elaborate social science experiments ever carried out in a natural setting" (1964:32).

In Taichung there were 36,388 married women in the prime reproductive age group out of a population (in 1963) of about 300,000 people. Four basic approaches were utilized to communicate information about birth control devices to these women. The researchers designated them as "Everything: wives and husbands," "Everything: wives only," "Mail," and "Nothing." The "Everything: wives and husbands" approach included posters, mailed literature, mass meetings, small group meetings,[15] and visits by public health nurses to both husbands and wives. The "Everything: wives only" approach was the same as the preceding except nurses visited only the wives. The "Mail" approach consisted of mass meetings, mailing of family-planning literature, and the use of posters. The "Nothing" approach involved only mass meetings and posters.

The city of Taichung is made up of 2,389 neighborhoods or *lin*'s, each having from twenty to thirty families. These *lin*'s were the basic units in the research. Approximately one third of the *lin*'s received the "Nothing" treatment, another one third received the "Mail" treatment, approximately one sixth received the "Everything: wives only" treatment, and the remaining one sixth received the "Everything: wives and husbands" approach. The *lin*'s were assigned to these various treatment conditions at random, although in the proper proportions.[16]

A basic hypothesis implicit in the study was that the more intense the campaign, the greater would be the rate of acceptance of family planning assistance. This may be broken down into six subhypotheses, as follows:

1. The "Everything: wives and husbands" approach would increase acceptance relative to the "Everything: wives only" approach;
2. The "Everything: wives and husbands" approach would increase acceptance relative to the "Mail" approach;
3. The "Everything: wives and husbands" approach would increase acceptance relative to the "Nothing" approach;
4. The "Everything: wives only" approach would increase acceptance relative to the "Mail" approach;
5. The "Everything: wives only" approach would increase acceptance relative to the "Nothing" approach;
6. The "Mail" approach would increase acceptance relative to the "Nothing" approach.

The basic paradigm employed in the study was the posttest-only version of the control-group paradigm. The tests of the six subhypotheses may be diagrammed as shown on pages 76–78.

---

[15] Small group meetings were inadvertently omitted in some cases.
[16] The random assignment of *lin*'s to treatments was subject to certain geographical constraints (see Berelson and Freedman 1964).

Sub-hypothesis 1

Treatment Group (*lin*'s which received the "Everything: wives and husbands" treatment)	R (random assignment of *lin*'s to Treatment Group)	X (receiving the "Everything: wives and husbands" treatment rather than the "Everything: wives only" treatment)	O (percentage of acceptances)
Comparison Group (*lin*'s which received the "Everything: wives only" treatment)	R (random assignment of *lin*'s to Comparison Group)		O (percentage of acceptances)

Sub-hypothesis 2

Treatment Group (*lin*'s which received the "Everything: wives and husbands" treatment)	R	X (receiving the "Everything: wives and husbands" treatment rather than the "Mail" treatment)	O
Comparison Group (*lin*'s which received the "Mail" treatment)	R		O

Sub-hypothesis 3

Treatment Group (*lin*'s which received the "Everything: wives and husbands" treatment)	R	X (receiving the "Everything: wives and husbands" treatment rather than the "Nothing" treatment)	O
Comparison Group (*lin*'s which received the "Nothing" treatment)	R		O

Sub-hypothesis 4

Treatment Group (*lin*'s which received the "Everything: wives only" treatment)	R	X (receiving the "Everything: wives only" treatment rather than the "Mail" treatment	O
Comparison Group (*lin*'s which received the "Mail" treatment)	R		O

Sub-hypothesis 5

Treatment Group (*lin*'s which received the "Everything: wives only" treatment)	R	X (receiving the "Everything: wives only" treatment rather than the "Nothing" treatment)	O
Comparison Group (*lin*'s which received the "Nothing" treatment)	R		O

Sub-hypothesis 6

Treatment Group (*lin*'s which received the "Mail" treatment)	R	X (receiving the "Mail" treatment rather than the "Nothing" treatment)	O
Comparison Group (*lin*'s which received the "Nothing" treatment)	R		O

The data relevant to these subhypotheses are summarized in Table 3.14. It can be seen that increased effort did not necessarily enhance the effectiveness of the program. Thus, the use of letters did not increase the acceptance rate for family-planning services and contacting both husband and wife was no more effective than contacting only the wife. However, one specific type of approach emerges as highly effective. Home visits by health workers to wives together with neighborhood small group meetings (the "Everything: wives only" treatment) did produce a marked increase in the utilization of family-planning services. Findings such as these are obviously of great practical importance as they enable those in charge of family-planning programs to channel limited funds into those activities most effective in promoting program goals.

TABLE 3.14 ACCEPTANCE RATES FOR CONTRACEPTIVE METHODS PER 100 MARRIED WOMEN AGED 20–39 IN TAICHUNG UP TO APRIL 1, 1964[a]

Treatment	Number of acceptors per 100 women
Everything: husband and wife	17
Everything: wife only	17
Mail	8
Nothing	8

[a] Adapted from Freedman and Takeshita (1969:126). Table VI-3. Reprinted by permission of Princeton University Press.

This research, of which only a small part has been summarized here, is impressive, both in its scope and in the general quality of its design and execution. The use of the control group paradigm makes it possible to discount a large number of rival hypotheses since it provides effective control over the major error sources.

There would seem to be no serious reliability and validity problems in the study. The dependent variable, acceptance of family-planning assistance, is operationally defined simply as "the insertion of an intrauterine device or the receipt of instructions and the purchase of supplies for other methods, together with expressed intent to practice contraception" (Berelson and Freedman 1964:34). Due to its simplicity and unequivocal nature, the measure seems likely to possess satisfactory reliability. It also features a very high degree of face validity.

The replicability of the study seems generally high, although it would be still further enhanced if additional details of the techniques used were made available —for example, the contents of the mailed materials and the format of the meetings.

A limitation of the data analysis in this study is the failure to make explicit use of statistical analysis in order to deal with the role of chance. While the observed differences between groups are of such a magnitude that it appears extremely unlikely they are due to chance, it would seem desirable to apply statistical tests of significance.

SUMMARY

As we have indicated previously in this chapter, hypothesis-testing research in anthropology has overwhelmingly relied, to date, on the static-group-comparison paradigm. More powerful paradigms that require premeasurements, such as the pretest–posttest and nonequivalent-control-group paradigms, have been quite rare.[17]

The prominence of the static group comparison in anthropological research appears to be the result of several factors. One reason is that many of the processes of interest to anthropologists are relatively long-term—that is, they operate over time spans of several human generations or longer. Examples of such long-term processes might include changes in kinship systems and religious ideology, adapta-

[17] One powerful paradigm, the postmeasurement-only version of the control-group paradigm, does not, of course, require premeasurements. It and the standard control-group paradigm do, however, require random assignment of cases and thus are unlikely to become widespread in anthropology, at least for the time being.

tion of cultural institutions to ecosystem features, or changes in child-training practices. When one attempts to test hypotheses involving very long term processes, there is perhaps little alternative to the use of a static group comparison since the premeasurements required in other paradigms often are not feasible. Another and related reason for the predominance of the static group comparison in anthropology is that the nature of certain sociocultural processes precludes premeasurements. We saw an example of such a process in Wolf's research on the relationship between infantile association and sexual attraction. A premeasurement paradigm would seem to have been unfeasible here due to the impossibility of obtaining a premeasure of sexual attraction from infants. When dealing with long-term processes and processes not amenable to premeasurement, then, the more powerful paradigms are generally precluded and the use of the static group comparison is unavoidable. As we have pointed out in reviewing the research by LeVine (1966) and Wolf (1970), special procedures may be used in many cases to partially compensate for the weaknesses of the static group comparison.

However, when we exclude from consideration long-term processes and processes inherently not amenable to premeasurement, we are left with a large number of intermediate and short-term sociocultural phenomena that would seem to lend themselves to study using powerful paradigms incorporating premeasurements. It is surprising, for example, that such paradigms have so rarely been used in studies of the short-term aspects of acculturation, modernization, and technological change, to give only a few of the more obvious examples.[18]

One of the more important reasons for the underutilization of the more powerful paradigms would seem to derive from existing conventions of anthropological field research. Field research in anthropology is conventionally done by means of relatively short-term, "one-shot" projects, often with a duration of a year or less. If premeasurement paradigms are to be applied, the research must encompass a long enough time span to "capture" the process of interest, that is, to permit measurements to be made both "before" and "after." Very many of the "short-term" processes of interest to anthropologists still have time spans measured in years rather than months or days—for example, the process of personality change that occurs in individuals who have moved from villages to cities. The study of phenomena such as this will obviously call for a lengthy research program that might take the form of an initial "baseline" study to obtain premeasurements and one or more additional studies over a period of several years in order to obtain postmeasurements. As long as anthropology continues to be wedded to the idea of the short-term, "one-shot" research program, the opportunities to apply powerful premeasurement paradigms will be severely and detrimentally circumscribed.

Of the paradigms requiring premeasurements, the pretest–posttest paradigm offers, perhaps, the smallest margin of benefit over the static group comparison.

---

[18] The reader familiar with the anthropological literature will be aware that the pretest–posttest paradigm has been employed to some extent in anthropological research on these topics. Generally, however, such studies have substituted for an actual premeasurement a *reconstructed premeasurement* based on informants' recollections of past events, historical documents, or, in some extreme cases, simply the researcher's imaginative powers. With certain exceptions, such "reconstructed" premeasures are extremely error-prone and are very difficult to quantify. For these reasons this version of the paradigm is not recommended.

This paradigm, while it avoids error due to selection, is quite subject to the effects of extraneous variables and reactive measurement effects. In the pretest–posttest paradigm, rival hypotheses concerning extraneous variables may be ruled out if the extraneous variables can be measured (as was shown above in our reivew of Festinger and Kelley's research). If, however, a great many extraneous variables are changing during the same period as the independent variable, it will be very difficult, if not impossible, to rule out rival hypotheses involving them. In such cases, the advantages to be gained from using this paradigm in preference to a simple static group comparison may be minimal.

Much to be preferred over either the pretest–posttest paradigm or the static group comparison is the nonequivalent-control-group paradigm. It not only is resistant to simple selection errors and reactive measurement effects, but also provides a great deal of control over extraneous variables. In situations where a pretest–posttest paradigm is feasible it is very often possible, with relatively little additional effort, to obtain a suitable comparison group as well, thus permitting the use of the nonequivalent-control-group paradigm. The advantages of this latter paradigm are so pronounced that it becomes virtually mandatory that the pretest–posttest paradigm be used only in situations where, for some reason, the nonequivalent-control-group paradigm is infeasible.

It is perhaps unlikely that the strongest of our paradigms, the control-group paradigm, will play a major role in anthropological research, at least in the near future; it is probable that anthropological research will continue to be characterized by commitment to the study of natural, on-going social systems where investigator intervention (which this paradigm generally requires) is undesirable and impracticable. The Lefkowitz et al. study (1955) does demonstrate, however, that it is sometimes possible to carry out research using a control-group paradigm within a natural social setting. And the study of fertility and birth-rates in Taiwan by Berelson and Freedman demonstrates a use of this paradigm that involved only minimal and relatively routine intervention by the investigators. Thus, it behooves anthropologists to be on the alert for situations in which this powerful paradigm may be applied in their research.

4 / The pragmatics of hypothesis-testing research in anthropology

Now that the elements of research design have been presented, both in general terms and by reference to examples (Chapters 2 and 3), we may turn to a discussion of the pragmatics of anthropological hypothesis-testing research. Pragmatic issues are those that can impede the researcher in his attempt to achieve the ideal represented by his research design. The major pragmatic issues to be discussed in this chapter are *site selection, sample selection*, and the *development of measures*. There is an additional pragmatic issue arising from the fact that research trends in anthropology have only recently begun to shift toward explanation and hypothesis-testing. The recency of this development can be expected to have an impact on students who are about to embark on their own fieldwork. They may well wonder, for example, where and how hypothesis-testing fits into the overall conception they have of traditional anthropological fieldwork. This very real pragmatic issue will be discussed in reference to the *timing* of anthropological fieldwork.

As presented here, these problems and issues will be related primarily to research that is to be conducted in a field situation.[1] Throughout this chapter, it will be assumed the anthropologist who is facing these pragmatic issues is already committed to conducting rigorous, hypothesis-testing research, and that he is familiar with the basic requirements for doing so. That is, it will be assumed he is familiar with the basic research paradigms (including their strengths and weaknesses) and with the other elements of a sound research design.

SITE SELECTION

Many considerations can enter into the selection of a research site but *primary* among these should be *the appropriateness of the site for an adequate test of one's hypotheses*. Sites differ greatly in ways that can be vital for the hypothesis-testing phase of fieldwork. Nevertheless, there are two factors of special importance. First, it is essential to pick sites where adequate numbers of cases may be found. If villages

---

[1] We will not, in this chapter, discuss the pragmatic issues associated with gathering and analyzing data for use in cross-cultural survey research (sometimes called hologeistic research). The pragmatics of this research are of a rather different type -and have been discussed at great length and with considerable clarity in a number of places, the most useful and accessible of these being Naroll and Cohen (1970), Naroll (1962) and Otterbein (1969).

are to be the cases, for example, the location chosen must be such as to provide access to the number of villages required for the study. Numerical adequacy of cases is important since, as noted in the discussion of sound research design, the rival hypothesis of chance must be taken into account. Generally this is feasible only if the number of cases is reasonably large. Although it is difficult to lay down general guidelines, ordinarily it is advisable to have at least twenty cases in any study, since in part the "power" of statistical tests rapidly decreases below this figure. However, many studies will call for substantially more cases and some may be done with fewer. A researcher unfamiliar with statistics will be well-advised to seek professional advice on the problem of the number of cases he will need *prior* to beginning his study.[2]

Second, it is vital to select a site where variation on the independent variable is found. Testing a hypothesis involves examining the independent and dependent variables to see if the relationship between them predicted by the hypothesis actually obtains. If there is no variation in the independent variable, it will be impossible to demonstrate either the presence or the absence of this relationship. To illustrate this, let us say a researcher wishes to test the hypothesis that multilineage villages (those populated by members of several different lineages) will tend to have village temples while monolineage villages (where all the inhabitants belong to the same lineage) will tend to lack them:

INDEPENDENT VARIABLE	NATURE OF RELATIONSHIP	DEPENDENT VARIABLE
Multilineage nature of village	increases the probability of	presence of village temple.

If the research site chosen happens to be an area where there is no variation on the independent variable—if either all villages are monolineage villages *or* all villages are multilineage—it will obviously be impossible to test the hypothesis, since there will be no way to ascertain whether multilineage villages indeed tend more to have temples than do monolineage villages.

It is often difficult, of course, to know in advance whether variation in the independent variable is to be found in a particular area. However, some evidence on the amount and kind of variation on particular variables in a given region may generally be obtained through searches of the ethnographic literature, consultations with persons familiar with the area, and examination of local archival material, such as newspapers and court records from the general area.

While the requirements of the research design are fundamental in site selection, it would be foolish to ignore the real possibility that more idiosyncratic considerations will play a part in the ultimate decision. This needs to be recognized so that, to all practical extents at least, these factors can be compared in importance to the more salient factors derived from the requirements of the research design. It may often be the case, for example, that sites will be selected because the essential financial support is available for one site and is unavailable for another. Frequently,

[2] For an excellent but relatively technical discussion of the number of cases necessary in research, see Hays 1965:329–333.

one's mentors and colleagues may be conducting research in a particular place and will in this way offer research opportunities that in effect "dictate" a choice of a site. Long-standing personal interests and training may similarly "dictate" choosing a site in South America say, over one in Oceania. Or, for the same reasons, the site may "have" to be in a city rather than a rural area (or vice versa). But in the final analysis, decisions about a field site should be influenced primarily by the major requirements of the research design, including the likelihood of variability on the independent and dependent variables and the availability of a sufficient number of cases to permit taking the role of chance into account.

SAMPLE SELECTION

As with the selection of a site, it is essential that the sample(s) be chosen with the requirements of the research design clearly in mind. For example, and as just noted, sample size needs to be sufficiently large to enable the use of statistical tests in analyzing the data. A second important aspect of sample selection is its *representativeness*. Every researcher must consider fully the importance for his research of the ability to *generalize* the results of his study to some larger population of cases. If this is important (and it often is), then the sample of cases *must* be selected with this goal in mind. From the standpoint of sampling, generalizability is dependent upon selecting a sample of cases that is representative of the larger population.

To illustrate the importance of obtaining a representative sample of cases if the results of a study are to be generalized to a larger population, we can make use of a hypothetical example. Let us imagine a study carried out by an anthropologist interested in ways to encourage peasants in a particular society to accept a new agricultural technique. He has formed the hypothesis that adoption of such an innovation will be accelerated if community leaders endorse the innovation:

INDEPENDENT VARIABLE	NATURE OF RELATIONSHIP	DEPENDENT VARIABLE
Endorsement by community leaders	increases	rate of adoption of an innovation.

Let us suppose the anthropologist is able to carry out a well-designed nonequivalent-control-group study to test this hypothesis, and further, that this study shows that adoption of the innovation was indeed significantly greater in communities where endorsement of the leaders was secured. Since the study was well designed, the anthropologist is relatively confident that it supports his hypothesis—in other words, that he can conclude with little risk of error that endorsement by community leaders did indeed act to increase the rate at which villagers adopted the innovation. Would he, however, be justified in expecting the relationship he found between leader endorsement and adoption of an innovation in the sample of villages used in his study to hold for the total population in which he is interested—that is, all the peasant communities in the society? The answer to this depends to a great extent on the representativeness of his sample. If his sample is highly representative (that is, if it closely resembles the larger population of villages in all major characteristics) then he can be relatively confident that any relationships he finds in his sample will also be found in the total population of villages, since his sample is in effect a microcosm of the entire population of villages in this society. If, however, his sample of villages is in some important way *non*representative of the total population of villages, it might well be the case that a relationship found in the sample will not obtain in the larger population of villages. Let us assume, for example, that the relationship between leader endorsement and adoption of innovations applies only to faction-free villages. In villages that are seriously factionalized, leader endorsement will not only fail to increase the rate of adoption but will actually impede it because the leaders of such villages are opposed by large numbers of villagers. Let us further assume that villages in this society are for the most part highly disorganized and faction-ridden, but the villages making up the sample studied by the researcher happened to be faction-free and were thus unrepresentative. In such a situation, the researcher would obviously be unjustified in generalizing the results of his study, carried out on an unrepresentative sample, to the total population of villages in which he is interested.

Given that the best assurance that one's results are generalizable to a larger population lies in the representativeness of one's sample, how can a researcher assure himself of a representative sample? The most satisfactory way is by *random sampling*—that is, by letting each case in the population have an equal chance of being included in the sample. If cases from the total population are included in the sample on a random basis, it is unlikely any particular type of case will be significantly over- or underrepresented in the sample. Thus, had the sample of villages used in the preceding example been selected from the total population by random means, it is highly unlikely that faction-free villages would have been significantly overrepresented in it. More likely, the proportion of faction-free villages in the sample would have been very close to the actual proportion of such villages in the population of villages.

While random sampling provides the highly important advantage of maximizing the chances that the sample of cases is similar in all respects to the population from which it was drawn, obtaining a random sample of cases from a population can often be a difficult procedure.

A convenient way of drawing a random sample is to assign numbers to the members of a population so that a table of random numbers can be used to select (or "draw") the sample on a random basis. An example of this is provided by the hypothetical research into the effects of initiation on *zoco* attacks (pp. 26–30). In field research, however, the population from which the sample is to be drawn frequently cannot be enumerated. In such cases, an *approximation* to a random sample may be obtained by dividing the population into roughly similar groups and randomly sampling from some of these groups. This is known as *cluster sampling*. To illustrate this, we may suppose a researcher desires to draw a random sample of adult males from a particular area but finds that no enumeration of males exists. He would thereby be precluded from drawing a pure random sample (unless, of course, he is willing to underwrite the expense of doing a census of the total area). He can, however, use cluster-sampling techniques to approximate a random sample. He may begin by selecting a random sample of villages from those in the area. He can then enumerate all the households in his sample villages and randomly select several households from each village. Finally, he can enumerate the male members in all the households selected and draw a random sample of these men to provide him with his final sample. These steps are shown in Fig. 4.1. The final sample of adult males he obtains will, as a rule, closely approximate the pure random sample he would have obtained by the much more expensive process of first enumerating all adult males in the area and then drawing a random sample from this list.[3]

Step 1   All villages in the area are enumerated and a random sample of villages is obtained.

Step 2   In each village selected in step one, all households are enumerated and a random sample of households is drawn from these villages.

Step 3   In each household selected in step two, all adult males are enumerated and a random sample of adult males is drawn. This will constitute the research sample.

FIG. 4.1   THE PROCESS OF DRAWING A SAMPLE OF ADULT MALES
BY CLUSTER SAMPLING TECHNIQUES

Anthropological sampling is often made extremely difficult because the cases (especially when they are people) resist being drawn into a sample and then "measured." In some instances, the random selection process itself has made people suspicious. Cohen (1973) found that local political leaders preferred to participate in the sample-selection process, thus making random selection impossible. These leaders insisted that selecting people at random would make them uncooperative. In such instances it may be necessary for the researcher to accept a judgmental sample—that is, a sample which is not randomly drawn but rather is selected by the researcher on the basis of his best judgment as to what would constitute a representative sample. In some extreme situations, the researcher may not even be able to select a sample on the basis of judgment but must accept a sample of convenience —must make do with whatever sample happens to be accessible.[4] The use of samples of doubtful representativeness, of course, makes it imperative that the researcher use utmost caution in generalizing the results he obtains from studying such a sample to a larger population. In general, the goal of randomly sampling the population of interest should not be too easily abandoned, as this technique provides the researcher with the best assurance that his sample is likely to closely resemble this population.

[3] See Mueller et al. 1970:357–362, however, for some cautions regarding the substitution of cluster-sampling for pure random sampling.

[4] Formerly, it was frequently held that statistical tests could not be legitimately applied to studies involving samples that were not strictly random. Recently, however, Winch and Campbell (1969) have provided a very powerful rationale for the application of these tests to research using other than random samples. The reader should also consult the following excellent sources for further details regarding the complex and vital matter of sampling: Blalock (1972), Cochran (1953), Hansen et al. (1953), Kish (1965), Moser and Kalton (1972), and Schuessler (1973).

DEVISING MEASURES

Despite its fundamental role in all science, the development of measures is still one of the most debated and underdeveloped facets of anthropology. This is not because anthropologists dislike taking elaborate steps to measure things (although no doubt there are those who do); rather, there is a strong tradition that views ethnographers themselves as the best tools for measuring. Often, the only advice regarding measurement given novices to anthropological fieldwork has been to take along an extra set of Rorschach cards, or a set of map-making tools, or a copy of *Notes and Queries on Anthropology* (1951).[5] Some of these tools may be worthwhile as the basis of certain kinds of measurement, but the principal justification for including a measure in one's array of field equipment should be its relevance to intended research, not simply its status as a traditional "thing to do."

Measurement of the independent and dependent variables is one of the most difficult and error-prone aspects of anthropological fieldwork, and yet it is also one of the most important. Every practical step that will increase the level of precision, the validity, and the reliability of the measures should be taken. Far more often than is indicated in traditional anthropological sources, some of these steps can be taken *prior* to leaving for the field.

The reader familiar with much of the available literature on anthropological fieldwork will recognize that our views diverge somewhat from those commonly encountered. Specifically, we do *not* share the view that it is generally best for the fieldworker to go to the field *without* a prepared questionnaire or other means of measuring the variables in which there is a research interest. The more orthodox view, which we have rejected, seems to have been promoted by the realization that measuring techniques useful in one culture may be impracticable in others. Measurement instruments, for example, that ask the informant to rate certain objects on a one-to-seven scale may be quite incomprehensible to an illiterate Tierra del Fuegan, despite their usefulness among American college students. The adherents of the traditional view would argue, if we understand them rightly, that since the anthropologist who develops (or adopts) a measure before leaving for the field is taking a risk that it may be ineffective in the field situation, he is well-advised to put off all consideration of measurement until he has become established in the field. We would certainly concede that there is some risk in taking developed measures to the field, especially if lavish amounts of time and money are allocated to their development. However, the risk in departing for the field without developed measures is, we would maintain, a far greater one, since failure to deal with the problem of measurement prior to leaving for the field has often meant that satisfactory measures were never attained and that the quality of the field research was therefore compromised. What is called for, we believe, is for the researcher to enter the field with predeveloped measures wherever possible *and* with the skills and equipment necessary to modify these measuring instruments or to develop new ones if the predeveloped measures prove unsatisfactory. Such a strategy, if adopted, would

[5] *Notes and Queries on Anthropology* is a famous volume prepared originally in 1874 as a guide to the fieldworker who intended to gather general descriptive data about a particular culture. Now in its sixth edition, the volume continues to be an important reference work for many anthropologists, though its value has been disputed for a variety of reasons.

necessarily require far more emphasis on measurement technique and theory than is found in the usual training program in anthropology. A comprehensive course of instruction in measurement for anthropologists should include, we would suggest, training in structured interviewing, survey questionnaire techniques, and those aspects of psychometrics most relevant to anthropology. Such a course should also, in our opinion, lay considerable stress on the use of "unobtrusive measures," which include, but are not limited to, conventional anthropological "participant observation" and which are often applicable in situations where other types of measures fail. The following section will briefly describe some less widely known unobtrusive measurement techniques, many of which we may expect to be useful in constructing anthropological measures.

Alternative Measurement Procedures

Anthropologists have for years relied upon "participant observation" as the principal means of measuring and describing whatever it is they have been interested in. It is to be expected that this method will be relied upon for some time to come, as well it should, since it can be a very effective procedure. On the other hand, anthropologists are turning more to methods adopted by other social scientists as they become increasingly interested in testing hypotheses. One such method, which can be very effective, is the survey questionnaire method. Most (if not all) Americans are familiar with survey questionnaires. Anthropologists are familiar with them, too, though they sometimes seem less patient with them than are most other Americans. The lack of emphasis in anthropology on the testing of hypotheses, the emphasis on participant-observation data-gathering methods, and the traditional view that taking questionnaires to the field is undesirable have combined to make the questionnaire a hotly disputed means for gathering anthropological data. Although we believe the disputants may have some strong arguments on their respective sides, we will not enter into the debate here.[6] Rather, we will review briefly some alternatives to both traditional anthropological participant observation on the one hand, and questionnaire surveys on the other, which can be used to gather the data needed to test hypotheses. In this review, we will rely heavily on the excellent summary of such alternative procedures provided by Webb, Campbell, Schwartz, and Sechrest (1966).

Their book, *Unobtrusive Measures*, is presented to encourage the social scientist to broaden his "currently narrow range of utilized methodologies and to encourage creative and opportunistic exploitation of unique measurement possibilities" (1966:1). They note that "some 90 per cent of social science research is based upon interviews and questionnaires." While questionnaires are a useful means of getting needed data, the authors of this important little book feel (as do we) that of the various weaknesses associated with the use of questionnaires, the principal one is that they are so often the *only* method used!

---

[6] Some of the problems of conducting survey research in areas of the world commonly studied by anthropologists are discussed in Glock (1967), Kish (1965), Frey (1969), Rokkan et al. (1969), and O'Barr et al. (1973).

Their book deals with a great variety of measuring techniques that, unlike questionnaires, do not depend upon a manifest or obvious approach on the part of the researcher. Rather, they depend upon the ingenuity of the researcher in discovering them, since they are subtle, not widely known and their utility varies greatly from place to place. The authors review five basic types of unobtrusive measures, giving numerous examples of each and noting their strengths and weaknesses.

The first major type they term the *physical trace measure*. These are the Sherlock Holmesian measures that depend upon making inferences from the physical remains of past human action. For example, a well-known car dealer in Chicago was able to determine which radio stations his customers listened to most often by having his repairmen keep a record of the station to which customers for repair work had tuned their radios. With the accumulated record of the physical traces of the past decisions of his many customers he was able to allocate his radio advertising budget accordingly. Similarly, an estimate of liquor sales in a dry town in Massachusetts was made by counting the number of empty liquor bottles in the town's trash. These and many similar unobtrusive physical trace measures can provide essential data for the test of anthropological hypotheses.

These measures offer the important advantage of being inconspicuous. As Webb and his colleagues put it (1966:50), "the stuff of analysis is material which is generated without the producer's knowledge of its use by the investigators." It is a form of measurement that is free from the problem of reactivity and would, therefore, be especially recommended when using research paradigms (such as the pretest–posttest paradigm) subject to this problem. There are, however, several disadvantages to such procedures. Not all physical traces of human behavior have the same survival rate. This is a problem of great significance and familiarity to the archaeologist. When other social scientists use such physical trace measures, the problem becomes theirs as well. Another drawback is that it is often difficult to know specifically which people produced the physical traces observed, although such information may be vitally needed. For example, while it may be possible to determine liquor sales volume by counting empty bottles in trash, it is not likely that this method would reveal who specifically was buying or drinking the liquor. Nevertheless, used in conjunction with other methods for obtaining data on the same variables, physical trace measures can prove to be very valuable.

The second type of unobtrusive measure discussed by Webb and his co-authors is termed the *archival, running record*. These are "data periodically produced for other than scholarly purposes, but which can be exploited by social scientists. These are the ongoing, continuing records of a society . . ." (1966:53). Once again, these measures are valuable because of their inconspicuousness. Since the data originally were produced for purposes other than those the social scientist has in mind, reactive measurement effects are less likely to occur. An example of the use of archival records to test an anthropological hypothesis was provided by Wolf's study (pp. 37–42), which employed birth records to develop a measure of sexual attraction between spouses. Archival records of potential use to anthropologists include actuarial, political, judicial, and government records, and the record provided by the various mass media (newspapers, magazines, and the broadcast media). While these records are potentially very valuable, they are subject to some significant weaknesses. Thus, as one anthropologist has pointed out (Naroll 1962), it is often difficult to assess the *quality* of archival data (in terms of accuracy, completeness, representativeness, and so forth). Records of this type can be biased in all sorts of ways, some intentional, most perhaps not. In any case, the effect is the same—the room for doubt is increased. But, as with the physical trace measures, the advantage of nonreactivity often can balance these defects, especially when archival material is used in conjunction with data collected in other ways.

The third type of measurement procedure they discuss is similar to the previous one. It is the *episodic private archival record*; that is, the record produced less regularly and perhaps unintentionally by other people for their own private or semi-private use. Examples are the sales records of stores, the records of institutions (hospitals, schools, and so on), and various kinds of personal documents (letters, suicide notes, diaries). As an example of the private institutional record, Webb et al. suggest that hotel and restaurant records could be used to provide data for a comparative study of occupations. For example, records on drink consumption and petty thievery in convention hotels ought to provide useful data about certain traits of different occupational groups. For example (1966:90), "Do anthropologists take more soap and towels away with them than do mechanical engineers?" Similarly, and perhaps more importantly, they note the possibility of checking sales records of bars around the United Nations as a measure of anxiety or tension during various key debates. These records, while less subject to the problem of varying decay rates, are weakened by their being potentially unrepresentative. Can it be assumed, for example, that the anthropologists who go to conventions represent their population in the same way that convention attending engineers represent theirs?

The fourth type of unobtrusive measure has been termed *simple observation*. Included here is the well-known and previously-noted method of participant observation, although it is only one of several such "simple" observational procedures they discuss. They mention and give examples of the utility of observing various physical signs (clothes, tatoos, and so on), personal, expressive mannerisms (body motions, kinesics,[7] and so on), physical-location observations, and various forms of time and duration sampling (such as the childhood behavior projects of Barker and Wright 1951 and 1954, and Whiting 1963). An illustration of one personal mannerism measure, albeit an informal one, is the waitress cited by Webb and his co-authors (1966:141) who observes (in song):

> I can tell that you're a logger,
> And not just a common bum.
> 'Cause nobody but a logger
> Stirs his coffee with his thumb.

In a more serious vein, they offer an example of the importance of making simple observations of physical location by reminding us of the significance of seating order at important political functions, or the possibility of making inferences about racial attitudes by noting voluntary seating behavior in racially mixed classrooms.

---

[7] Kinesics is the study of body motions and communication, a field pioneered by the anthropologist Ray L. Birdwhistell (1970).

Often the examples they give depend upon the making of observations without the subjects becoming aware that they are in fact under the watchful eye of the researcher. Used carefully, such techniques, like most of the others mentioned, are unobtrusive and thus avoid the problem of reactive measurement effects. As anthropologists are well aware, direct observation permits more subtle assessments about the individuals who produce various forms of behavior than do physical trace and archival methods. Thus, it might be more meaningful to watch people buying liquor and drinking it than to count empty bottles in trash cans. Decisions about such matters will have to be made in terms of the requirements of one's research goals.

However, while the direct observation method does offer numerous important advantages, it is subject to some very serious drawbacks. Probably the most serious of these is observer bias. It has been shown on numerous occasions and in numerous ways that observers, especially those who are testing hypotheses, have great difficulty in maintaining acceptable standards of objectivity and reliability throughout the research project. Changes in observer objectivity are known, picturesquely enough, as *observer decay*, and this effect is a very serious problem in anthropology where so much research has traditionally been based on direct participant observation. Though it is seldom done in anthropology, reliability estimates can—and should where feasible—be made to estimate the extent of the bias arising from observer decay. However, when observation is conducted by a single person, as is generally the case in traditional anthropological fieldwork, such a reliability check is virtually impossible. This fact alone is a strong argument favoring the use of measuring techniques less subject to observer decay or dependent on the use of more than one observer so that reliability checks can be made. A second source of error affecting simple observational measures is the problem of reactive measurement effects. The very presence of an observer can alter behavior in ways that can render the data collected biased and inaccurate. We have noted this problem in general when discussing measurement reactivity and have suggested that research designs which control this problem somewhat should be utilized when the measures are likely to be reactive.

The fifth type of measurement is the *contrived observation*. This type of measure has been used more in sociology and psychology than in anthropology, though there is good reason to expect this situation will change. Contrived measures are those that the researcher makes after having induced people to participate in some observed activity, or that are made by an observer using hidden equipment. We have already noted an example of one type of contrived measure when we described (page 23) the attempt by Mischel to estimate the ability of children to defer gratification. He offered them, you will recall, a choice between a big candy bar later or a small one right away. Other more elaborate procedures have been developed, including the use of hidden microphones, sensing devices, and cameras. These measurement procedures offer the advantages of minimizing observer effects and, since the recording of the data is often mechanical, enhancing reliability.

In all these unobtrusive measurement procedures, however, there is a potentially significant problem that needs to be made most explicit. For some anthropologists, these unobtrusive methods (and especially the contrived, hidden measures), may pose a significant ethical problem. In extreme forms, such measures can give the appearance of *1984* come early. Generalizations about the ethical implications of these measurement procedures cannot be made easily (if at all) since there are so many different unobtrusive measures. However, the authors of the book *Unobtrusive Measures* do note the importance of the ethical implications of the methods they describe, and they urge that anyone contemplating their use become fully sensitized to the potential dangers. Nevertheless, they also note (as would we) that taken to an extreme, *any* measurement technique can become unethical if it results in invasions of privacy or has other undesirable effects. It is, therefore, unwarranted to make blanket indictments of a large category of measures simply because a few, if taken to extremes, may be ethically undesirable. Rather, the consideration that must be made, both by individual researchers and the various social science professions, is the standards to apply in a given situation.

TIMING AND THE FIELDWORK PROCESS

The image of the lone anthropologist, in a remote corner of the world, struggling against the elements in order to collect data on the lifeways of an obscure population, is well established and unlikely to disappear very soon. This image has tended to foster the view that fieldwork is a mystical rite which must be endured alone and with a stoicism equaled only, perhaps, by the vision quests of Native Americans. But we believe, as do many other anthropologists, that this view is just what it has been thought to be—an *image* which does not reflect the reality experienced by most anthropologists. Of course, virtually any anthropologist can regale students with exciting and awesome anecdotes about the rigors of fieldwork. But these stories, while perhaps no less common now than in the past, are certainly becoming less important as an indication of the success of the fieldwork (or of the anthropologist).

However, since the image is likely to remain with us, can we expect students to ignore it when they begin to plan their own research? We think not, and thus we will turn now to a discussion of the place of hypothesis-testing research in the context of "traditional" anthropological fieldwork.

Experience suggests that most anthropological fieldwork, whether undertaken by an individual over a period as short as a few months, or by a team of people over a period as long as several years, can be divided into five *overlapping* phases. These are (1) predeparture preparation, (2) initial "settling-in" period, (3) description and context assessment, (4) final reassessment of the research design, and (5) data collection and analysis. It must be stressed immediately that these five phases are only intended as a general characterization of the fieldwork process. In specific research projects, one or several of these phases may be subdivided, or altered in other ways. For example, the length of these phases may vary considerably from one research project to another, so that one or more of them may be very prominent while others are barely detectable. Nevertheless, these phases are sufficiently common to warrant some discussion of them here. This is especially justified in view of traditional anthropological conceptions of some of these phases, which, for the person interested in testing hypotheses, may be outmoded and misleading conceptions.

Predeparture Preparations

All anthropologists undergo considerable general training before actually entering the field. Conventional anthropological wisdom has reinforced the notion that fieldwork is something of an initiation rite or a mystical experience for which total preparation is almost impossible. To be sure, a thorough grounding in the literature of anthropology is stressed. But all too often there has been little in the way of careful planning of the research prior to undertaking it. This deplorable state of affairs in anthropology may be attributed to the rather pronounced emphasis—still surviving today, in some quarters—on what must be described as a natural history approach to research. That is, it was widely assumed until recently that descriptive statements about the behavior and thoughts of other people constituted the primary concern of anthropology. Moreover, it was often assumed that making such statements required primarily a sensitive person who knew the anthropological literature and who had the means to support himself while he lived for an extended period among the people whose behavior and thoughts he wished to describe. Throughout the history of anthropology, there have been many whose fieldwork projects have been far more sophisticated than this. But this view of anthropological fieldwork has been strong enough to produce relatively serious deficiencies in predeparture preparations.

For example, it is widely heard advice that one should not enter the field with well-developed hypotheses, questionnaires, and other measuring instruments, or a fully developed set of expectations about the aims of the research. The pressures of granting agencies (which do not share these anthropological conceptions of fieldwork and who hold all-important purse-strings) have undermined these tendencies somewhat, but there are still anthropologists who strongly support these images. In stressing the need for predeparture preparations, we are not taking the position that anthropologists should assume they can exclude serendipity from their fieldwork. That an important but unexpected development will emerge during fieldwork is probably one of the few certainties in anthropological research; moreover, serendipitous events have been important to all the sciences. But this is true only when the researcher is well prepared and knows how to take advantage of these developments. What we are saying is that almost total reliance on chance happenings or on related underlying assumptions of much anthropological fieldwork (such as, "There's a lot of culture 'out there' and I'll certainly find something important to study.") is unacceptable practice now.

Thus, contrary to other guidelines for the fieldworker, we would urge that the student of anthropology place special emphasis on certain specific predeparture preparations. In particular, we recommend giving more attention to developing hypotheses, potential measures of the key variables, and the development of the strongest feasible research paradigm.

The development of hypotheses at this early stage is essential for successful fieldwork. Indeed, it would be our contention that their development is vital to the justification for expending the large amounts of time and money that will ordinarily be required for most extended fieldwork. A factor that must be considered in developing hypotheses is the availability of the resources necessary to support the collection of the data required to put the hypotheses to an adequate test. Thus, it will be necessary to review the hypotheses, noting which few of the many potentially interesting ones may be adequately tested with the resources available. Hypotheses can be differentiated in terms of their importance to theory building, in that some, when tested, will provide more information or more vital information than others. For example, hypotheses that emerge from conflicting bodies of theory may be important to test if, in testing them, the points of disagreement can be resolved or modified. Some hypotheses may have a special relevance to practical issues of interest to the researcher or to the people being studied. For example, in the hypothetical study of village cohesion described in Chapter 2, there could well be considerable local concern over the long-range effects of the introduction of the windmills if and when they are introduced into other areas. If empirical evidence is made available regarding those effects, then appropriate corrective measures can be more readily developed.

The development of a research paradigm ought to be one of the more routine predeparture tasks. The various research paradigms have been described and their weaknesses and strengths are known. In instances where less powerful research paradigms must be used, plans should then be made to provide as many checks as possible against rival hypotheses.

Initial Settling-in Period

The first days of a prolonged period of anthropological fieldwork in a foreign country, or amongst people with cultures different from that of the fieldworker's can be among the most crucial of all. Culture shock, illness, tension, and uncertainty are as likely to be characteristic of this period as are excitement, adventure, pleasure, and intellectual illumination.

Whatever their reactions, researchers should not permit them to obscure the fact that this period is vitally important to later efforts to test hypotheses. In an earlier section, we discussed the importance of taking great care in choosing a site for research; however, most fieldworkers, no matter how careful they have been, will have based their site decision on information that almost certainly will be a little dated by the time they actually arrive in the field. Because the characteristics of a site are so important, it is advisable that during this initial period, the sites again be reviewed carefully. Before making the final commitment to the research site, all the requirements of the research design which can be affected by the characteristics of the site should be checked to ensure that the site ultimately selected is indeed adequate. Care in making decisions about where one will live, work, and conduct one's hypothesis-testing research cannot be too great, and the initial settling-in period, while generally associated with a variety of activities, is an ideal time to make that all-important final check.

A major concern of this phase of the research has been termed "impression management" by some anthropologists (e.g., Berreman 1962 and Pelto 1970). The term is reasonably descriptive, although it may be somewhat misleading in its Madison Avenue overtones. Observations of modern American domestic political campaign strategies (especially "image-making") as well as accounts of experience abroad suggest how important one's hosts' first impressions can be for longer-range goals related to fieldwork. The way one walks, talks, dresses, eats—and the list here is almost endless—can convey a great deal of information to other people. No group of professional social scientists is more aware of this than anthropologists. It is not surprising, then, that they pay a great deal of attention to the effect of impressions made during the early days and weeks in the field.

Nothing is more disheartening to the fieldworker, for example, than closed doors, turned faces, disinterested eyes, or silent mouths. These all-too-common responses do not necessarily come from general fear or hostility on the part of the host people but often result from certain subtle (especially to the outsider) cues in one's personal behavior. Of all the areas where guidance may be needed, this is perhaps one of the most pressing, but ironically it is the least amenable to general advice. Nevertheless, there should be no difficulty in seeing the link between this facet of the first few days in the field and the likelihood of successfully undertaking any of the later phases of the research. Indeed, the consequences of "impression management" are probably never so great as during the hypothesis-testing phase of the research. The most common reason for this is linked to measurement and sample selection. Both of these fundamental steps in hypothesis-testing research ordinarily will require the cooperation and participation of large numbers of people—certainly larger numbers than had been involved in any of the other phases of the research. As we have noted, problems associated with these steps can be formidable under the best of circumstances; poor impression management in the settling-in phase will generally only complicate them further.

We would hasten to add, however, that as vital as these first days can be, it is nevertheless the case that people do not always hold "grudges" throughout one's entire fieldwork because of innocent mistakes in behavior during the early days of the fieldwork. Indeed, for some anthropologists such mistakes have often been the basis for considerable humor rather than for serious concern. Unnecessary anxiety over this important period can itself provoke more difficulties than might have otherwise been the case. Hence our caution in using the slightly loaded term "impression management." Gaining some amount of community acceptance is important, to be sure, but excessive anxiety about impression management may produce unnatural or uncharacteristic responses that, in addition to being uncomfortable for the anthropologist, will increase the likelihood of undesirable reactions or other negative and unwanted complications.[8]

Finally, we would note that it has been recommended (for example, by Williams 1967) that this initial period of the fieldwork is an excellent time to conduct surveys, map-making tours, and the like, since these are often routine activities. Experience varies on this point, of course, but many have found that these surveys are neither so routine nor so benign as Western researchers tend to view them. For that reason alone, then, this activity could justifiably be relegated to a later phase of the fieldwork. But there are additional grounds for this suggestion. Two of the later phases of the research (description and context assessment, and final reassess-

---

[8] The problem of entry into the field is discussed by four of the contributors to the volume on anthropological methods edited by Naroll and Cohen (1970). These problems as they pertain to New Guinea are discussed by L. L. Langness; to Africa by John Middleton; to a Navajo community by Victor C. Uchendu; and to Arctic and Subarctic North America by James W. VanStone.

ment of the research design) may well yield important new avenues of inquiry. Following-up on these leads may be impractical if extensive effort has already been devoted to surveys conducted during the early settling-in period of fieldwork. These late but important developments can have an important bearing on the testing of hypotheses and should not be neglected. Adequate predeparture preparation of schedules can serve to guard against this unwarranted but nevertheless understandable urge to get on with the research. Strategic pacing in the early phases of the fieldwork can enhance results during subsequent data-collection and analysis phases.

Description and Context Assessment

There is a prevalent image—or rather, a caricature—of anthropologists who are committed to hypothesis-testing research that is plausible enough to have been widely accepted as fact, rather than the fancy it is. This is the image of the naive anthropologist interested in testing a hypothesis who, with questionnaire in hand, rushes into the field, draws a sample of cases, asks his questions, and rushes off again. It cannot be stressed too strongly how unwise such a procedure generally is. Such an approach, on the face of it, falls so far short of the mark, as regards the care and preparation associated with sound research, that it is not at all surprising the image is looked upon with such disfavor. However, an uncritical and perhaps traditional response to this image is also of questionable value, at least for hypothesis-testing research. This is the traditional assumption that anthropological fieldwork must, as a nearly unbreakable rule, include a long period of exploratory, descriptive research. Such an assumption can be questioned, but in doing so it should be noted carefully that we are not suggesting that the anthropologist interested in testing hypotheses should ignore this important aspect of all research. Rather, we would urge that description, like all other research activity, be seen in a perspective appropriate for the research in question.

For many, description has been the principal goal of anthropological fieldwork. Indeed, much anthropological fieldwork never really gets beyond this stage. Such efforts are often analogous, at their most basic level, to salvage archaeology or natural history—both are important strategies, but neither represent the highest possible goals of their respective disciplines. Several factors lie behind this situation—and the analogy. First, anthropologists know, or at least believe, that the data "out there" are valuable. At the very least, they know that if the data aren't collected *now*, they will be gone forever. Second, some anthropologists are convinced it is better to get what can be gotten, put it into whatever boxes or pigeonholes are available, label them as best one can, and store them in the basement of a museum or in an ethnological archive until such time that the material can be reexamined for purposes of testing one or another hypothesis. There can be no doubt that this practice and philosophy continues to be (and should be) important in anthropology, but there *can* be doubt about the wisdom of this as the dominant practice. An increasing number of anthropologists are coming to share Anthony Wallace's view (1970:4) that "ethnographic description, like daily weather reporting, is an endless task" and they have, therefore, begun to question whether description can or should be an end in itself.

At the same time, however, it would be an error of the most serious proportions to conclude from this that exploratory research and description are irrelevant for hypothesis-testing research in anthropology. On the contrary, this criticism of the traditional emphasis on description reflects our view that description should be a means to an end—that end being testing hypotheses *and* building theory. The point is that the *context* of the research, presented by means of ethnographic description, provides a vital dimension to the analysis. This added contextual dimension provides a perspective that can help to minimize interpretive errors regarding the hypothesis related data—errors so often noted by anthropologists when examining the work of colleagues in such related disciplines as sociology and psychology. We would also stress, however, that this knowledge of the cultural context should be acquired *before* the data necessary for the tests of the hypotheses central to the research are collected. This general recommendation makes it possible to bring relevant, newly acquired, cultural insights to bear on the evaluation of the design of the hypothesis-testing phase of the research.

Thus, in general, it can be expected that hypothesis-testing research will of necessity include some efforts which are designed to provide the appropriate cultural context material. The more of this material that can be obtained during the predeparture preparation phase of the fieldwork, the shorter this activity is likely to be in the field. In the past, anthropologists tended to seek places to conduct their research that had not previously been the subject of their colleagues' enquiring eyes. This tendency continues to the present day, as a preference at least, and to a considerable extent as a reality. But we may expect that as time passes there will be an increasingly large number of researchers who will be undertaking fieldwork in areas where the "basic ethnography" is already available; that is, where the cultural context has been given at least a basic assessment by an anthropologist. In such circumstances, it is to be hoped (if not assumed) the researcher will familiarize himself as thoroughly as possible with the cultural context data prior to leaving for the field. Then, while in the field, and during the "descriptive and context assessment phase," these understandings can be updated and checked with current local conditions. Finally, it should be noted that in discussing the selection of a site, it was assumed that some effort, hopefully a thorough one, would be made to assess the various potential sites in terms of research design needs. Doing this would necessarily involve gathering data regarding some aspects of cultural context.

Final Reassessment of the Research Design

This often-ignored phase of anthropological fieldwork is one of the most important of all, especially for those attempting to test hypotheses.

Information acquired during the context assessment phase of field research may point up serious inadequacies in the research design or serious practical obstacles to its implementation. It is therefore imperative that *all* aspects of the research design be reevaluated at this juncture. The feasibility of the various paradigms must be reviewed and appropriate changes made. Similarly, the measures of the independent and dependent variables, the determination of the nature of the cases, and the drawing of samples should be reconsidered in the light of insights gained during the descriptive, context-assessment phase. This might mean that the number of hypotheses will increase (or perhaps decrease, though this seems less likely), and the measurements will have to be altered in order to take local conditions into account. In any case, we can assume that the input of data from the descriptive phase will generally influence the specific features and content of the research design but will not alter the basic principles by which designs are constructed and evaluated.

Data-Gathering and Analysis Phases

It is during these two phases that many additional pragmatic issues arise—for example, whether or not to pay informants, the training and use of interviewers and other kinds of research assistants, whether or not to use an interpreter, which of the various kinds of statistical methods to use, whether or not to utilize one or another kind of scoring system for analyzing the data, and so forth. These are problems frequently, and generally quite adequately, discussed in manuals on anthropological fieldwork,[9] and on general statistics and data analysis. We will not therefore discuss these problems here. We would emphasize, however, that these problems are often unnecessarily encumbered by the utilization of an inadequate or poorly executed research design. For example, it will be difficult to gather data if insufficient attention has been given to the selection of a site or the development of workable measures. Similarly, it will be difficult to analyze the data adequately if insufficient attention has been given to the selection of a sample of cases that is adequate in terms of size and representativeness. Thus, while the specific pragmatic issues often discussed in connection with anthropological fieldwork are important, they will be worth solving only if and when the other basic features of a structurally and pragmatically sound research design have been fully considered.

---

[9] The volumes by Beattie (1965), Spindler (1970), and Williams (1967) in the series in which this volume appears are useful in this regard; other useful books are those by Pelto (1970), Jongmans and Gutkind (1967), and Freilich (1970).

5 / Summary and some general implications

In this book we have attempted to provide guidelines for designing and evaluating anthropological hypothesis-testing research. We will now reiterate the main points of the previous chapters, both as a summary and as a prelude to a more extended discussion of the implications of these views for the anthropological endeavor—in particular for such issues as the nature of anthropological research, the "emic-etic" debate, and research ethics.

EXPLANATION IN ANTHROPOLOGY

A crucial step in the explanation of human behavior is the ability to specify what conditions give rise to some other conditions (Rudner 1966:59). Making such explanatory statements depends on the development and test of *hypotheses* which may be defined, correspondingly, as tentative statements of what conditions will give rise to what other conditions. Testing a hypothesis involves exposing it to a situation that can show it to be false. If it survives such a test our confidence in it increases. However, research oriented to the test of hypotheses regarding human behavior is made difficult by numerous *sources of error* that must be dealt with if we are to explain human behavior. These error sources make it difficult to say with confidence that a particular set of conditions (an independent variable or variables) gives rise to (causes, produces), the phenomenon of interest (the dependent variable). It is difficult, in other words, to say that *this* set of conditions and not some other set caused or was a contributing cause of some particular human behavior. This is not because the causes of human behavior are inherently or uniquely ambiguous. Rather, it is difficult to conduct hypothesis-testing research that successfully controls the common sources of error to which such research is subject. Where these errors are not controlled, the investigator will face numerous *interpretive ambiguities*. That is, he will be unable to determine whether the results reflect the operation of the variables incorporated into his hypothesis or the operation of various sources of error.

RESEARCH DESIGN

Research is designed in ways that are intended to provide maximum protection against the effects of sources of error that lead to interpretive ambiguity. But not all research is equally sound simply because it has been "designed." In terms of the extent to which sources of error have been controlled, some designs are better than others. A principal goal of all researchers interested in testing hypotheses must be the identification and utilization of the best possible research design. And similarly, a principal goal of all those interested in reading and evaluating the hypothesis-testing research of others is the identification of the research design used and, consequently, of the kinds of errors to which the research may have been subject. Neither of these goals can be achieved if the researcher or reader is unfamiliar with the structure of the various research designs, and especially with the component parts of a design.

A research design has several major components. Of these, perhaps the most vital, in terms of reducing or eliminating sources of error, is the *research paradigm*. This is the element of the design that structures or patterns the measurement of variables. There are many possible research paradigms. In this book, we have discussed four very common ones: the *pretest–posttest* paradigm, the *static-group-comparison* paradigm, the *nonequivalent-control-group* paradigm, and the *control-group* paradigm. We have also noted a number of variations on these paradigms that are in common use. Both the basic paradigms and the variants were illustrated by examples in Chapter 3.

We have emphasized these four research paradigms because (in addition to being in common use) once the researcher is familiar with their structure he may more systematically identify the most common error sources or rival hypotheses. The structures of the various paradigms are closely associated with the various sources of error. There are three fundamental structural characteristics to be noted in these paradigms: whether or not the paradigm includes (1) a measurement of the dependent variable *prior* to the operation of the independent variable; (2) a comparison or control group that receives a low amount of (or exposure to) the independent variable, and (3) a procedure whereby the cases being studied are randomly assigned to the groups receiving high and low exposure to the independent variable. A paradigm with all three of these basic structural features is very powerful because the effects of major rival hypotheses are minimized. Only the standard control-group paradigm does, in fact, incorporate all three of these features. The three remaining basic paradigms incorporate various combinations of these features but not all of them. As a consequence, these three do not offer control over all the major error sources. The types of interpretive ambiguities that result from their use are linked to the structure of the paradigm; they are *not* random and unknown. Hence, it is possible to determine the type of weaknesses to which a particular research effort, using a particular paradigm, will be subject. Once these are known, the investigator can take steps to guard against them, either by using a different and more powerful paradigm (if this is possible) or by utilizing various statistical and analytical means to minimize interpretive ambiguity.

Four types of paradigm-related error sources (or rival hypotheses) that increase interpretive ambiguities are especially common and serious. These were discussed at length in Chapter 2. Briefly, they are (1) reactive measurement effects, (2) selection effects—that is, differences between groups due to the way they were selected, (3) effects of extraneous variables, and (4) effects due to the interaction of selection effects with other factors (such as extraneous variables). The susceptibility of the basic research paradigms to these error sources was summarized in Table 2.1; it is reproduced again here as Table 5.1. By examining this table the reader should be able to determine the effect of the presence or absence of one or more paradigm features on the control of the basic sources of error. For example, not having a comparison group makes it difficult (if not impossible) to control for the effects of extraneous variables.

TABLE 5.1   SOURCES OF ERROR[a]

Type of paradigm	Selection	Reactive measurement effects	Effects of extraneous variables	Interaction effects involving selection
Pretest–posttest		−	−	
O X O				
Static-group-comparison	−	+	+[b]	−
X O				
O				
Nonequivalent-control-group	+	+	+[b]	−
O X O				
O O				
Control-group	+	+	+	+
R O X O				
R O O				

[a] A minus indicates a weakness in regard to the source of error. A plus indicates the paradigm is resistant to the source of error. A blank indicates the source of error is not applicable to the paradigm.
[b] The static-group and nonequivalent-control-group paradigms are resistant to the effects of extraneous variables to the extent that these variables affect both groups in the same manner.

The research paradigm is not, however, the only component of a research design. We discussed three other basic elements. These are (1) the nature of the measurements employed, (2) the precautions taken against the role of chance, and (3) the provisions made to maximize the replicability of the research. In any test of a hypothesis, a central task is the development of a way to measure the dependent variable; sometimes it is also desirable to measure the independent variable. Of special importance are the validity, reliability, and precision of the measures. As is the case with research paradigms, and most other aspects of research design, not all measures are equally sound. The researcher must strive to obtain measures that can be shown to be *reliable* (the measure will give similar results when repeatedly used in the same circumstances), *valid* (the measure truly measures what it is intended to measure), and reasonably *precise* (the measure will make as many distinctions as are feasible regarding the amount or degree of the phenomenon to be measured).

Once the variables have been measured and the analysis of the results has begun, it is essential that the researcher consider yet another rival hypothesis—the role of chance. It is possible for errors in sampling, instabilities in measures, and other chance factors to occur even under the most rigorous research conditions. Changes in the dependent variable may thus be the result of chance rather than of the independent variable. Fortunately, there are procedures available for estimating the likelihood that chance has entered the picture to a serious degree. It is highly desirable that all hypothesis-testing research designs include a means of making this assessment. Although this step is widely recognized as necessary at the final analysis stage of the research, it is less widely understood that unless the research design includes certain characteristics at the outset, it may be impossible to rule out the effects of chance. A key factor in dealing with the role of chance is ensuring that the group or groups used in the research include a reasonably large number of cases. The necessary number of cases varies but usually will be at least 20 and often will be much larger. Finally, in hypothesis-testing research it is essential to provide sufficient information about all procedures used so that others can replicate the research and confirm the findings.

At the conclusion of Chapter 2, we listed four questions the researcher or reader ought to ask about any hypothesis-testing research. Ideally, he should be able to answer these questions affirmatively. After identifying the research paradigm used (or about to be used), the following questions are appropriate:

1) Is the research paradigm used the strongest possible one under the circumstances?
2) Do the measurements appear to be satisfactory with regard to their reliability, validity, and precision?
3) Have provisions been made for dealing with the role of chance?
4) Is the execution of the research described in such a way as to be replicable?

If these questions cannot be answered affirmatively, there is cause for concern about the design, and there may be grounds for doubt about the conclusions drawn (or about to be drawn) from the research. If the researcher asks these questions *before* undertaking the research, negative responses will hopefully be taken as indications of areas of the research design that are deficient and that require, therefore, some rethinking and adjustment.

RESEARCH PRAGMATICS

There are several pragmatic issues that, although technically not a part of the research design, can have a great deal to do with the overall success of anthropological fieldwork which is oriented to the test of hypotheses. In this book, we have discussed four of these pragmatic issues: (1) selecting a research site, (2) choosing a sample, (3) developing measures, and (4) timing.

In anthropology, selection of a research site has traditionally been the result of a complex interplay of personal and professional factors. This is perhaps unavoidable, but we would encourage anyone who is selecting a site for hypothesis-testing research to reach this key decision by making all determining factors as explicit as possible. If this is done, the relative salience of all these factors can be more readily considered. We believe the principles of sound research design argue persuasively for placing the design requirements at the head of the list of salient factors. This means, in effect, that a site must be selected only if it contains enough cases appropriate for the research in question, and that the site must be one the researcher has good reason to believe will provide substantial variation on the independent variable, for if there is no variation on the independent variable no test of the hypothesis is possible.

Devising measures has long been one of the thorniest problems in the social sciences. It probably has been most thorny for anthropologists. This problem grows out of the difficulty anthropologists have faced in attempting to learn merely the basic details of a culture, let alone measure them in a precise manner. Ironically, the realities of this situation have contributed to the development of a semisacred tradition in anthropology against the utilization (or even the encouragement) of precise measuring techniques. For those interested in the testing of hypotheses, this tradition, if followed, can be disastrous. Consequently, in discussing the pragmatics of hypothesis-testing research in anthropological field settings, we insisted that the development of measures of greater precision than has been typical of anthropological research in the past must be a high-priority goal. In saying this, however, we realize that many anthropologists will have visions of the questionnaire-toting survey researcher who will rush headlong into a field situation for a short period while he collects "quantified data" in order to test a hypothesis. Because of such images, there has been in the past a tendency for anthropologists to argue that fieldworkers should not enter the field with developed measures. We do not believe this to be the best response to the serious problem posed by poorly trained survey researchers. It makes a serious problem worse, because going to the field without considerable advance preparation (including, usually, trial measures of the sort one intends to attempt to use) has often made it difficult if not almost impossible for the fieldworker to develop adequate measurement procedures. Consequently, while we have suggested taking developed measures to the field, we have also stressed the very real need to take along the tools and skills necessary to alter the measures to suit the local conditions. Also, we have given considerable attention to the need to develop and utilize other measures besides the increasingly popular survey questionnaire. These measures, which include archival data and physical trace measures, were discussed in the previous chapter and were drawn extensively from the book, *Unobtrusive Measures* (Webb et al. 1966). For many anthropologists, some or all of these suggestions will undoubtedly have been notable more for their similarities to the basic and time-honored technique of participant observation than for any other characteristics they may have (and indeed, there are many such similarities). But we have emphasized the views of the authors of that book because it is too often assumed that the development of precise measures, which clearly is an advantage to be sought by the researcher, necessarily calls for the abandonment of participant observation. This view, while common, is incorrect. Adopting a concern for hypothesis-testing research does not mean that participant observation techniques must be abandoned; rather, efforts will have to be made to show that these techniques have produced or have the potential to produce reliable, valid, and reasonably precise data. This may require a great deal of creativity on the part of the anthropological fieldworker, but the theoretical and practical rewards should certainly be adequate compensation.

Selecting a sample is a process that often has been one of the biggest mysteries and stumbling blocks associated with anthropological research. If a researcher expects to generalize his results with any degree of confidence to any population that is larger than the sample, his sample must be representative of the larger population. The most satisfactory way of attaining representativeness is random sampling (although as we have noted, it is not infallible). This often proves difficult, especially in areas of the world where the population is not enumerated. We have noted, therefore, that in such areas the technique of cluster sampling (or some variant of it) provides an acceptable approximation to pure random sampling which is likely to be more feasible.

Finally, we noted a pragmatic implication that emerges because widespread interest in hypothesis-testing field research in sociocultural anthropology is a relatively recent development. For many people, a key issue of this recent development will be to determine how hypothesis-testing fieldwork fits into the context of what has come to be known as "traditional anthropological fieldwork." That is, can hypothesis-testing research be accommodated within the prolonged field project with general and primarily descriptive aims? For some, the answer may seem to be that it cannot. However, we have suggested some ways in which an accommodation may be reached. We have urged, first of all, that in the predeparture phase of fieldwork, a great deal more stress be placed on drawing up a comprehensive research design —which would, of course, include devising possible measures. We have also urged that the requirements of this design should be a prime consideration in selecting the precise site in which the research will be conducted. Finally, we have noted that the emphasis in the traditional fieldwork model on acquiring first-hand familiarity with the cultural context is highly compatible with hypothesis-testing research, since it may bring to light numerous conditions which will require alteration and elaboration of the research design, and it may provide the data needed to avoid overly provincial interpretations of the results.

IMPLICATIONS

The principles discussed in this book have many implications for the anthropological endeavor. Some of these have been noted in previous chapters. We have urged that greater efforts be made to utilize more powerful paradigms in place of the widely used static group comparison, a paradigm that has a number of serious weaknesses. This will mean, in many cases, that anthropologists should undertake longer research projects, lasting several years or more, so that the premeasurements required by these more powerful designs can be made.

Nevertheless, we also recognize that there may be restrictions which will make it virtually impossible for a single researcher to undertake research of such lengthy duration. Under such circumstances, and with the numerous critical comments made in discussing the examples in Chapter 3 clearly in mind, a reader might well ask the following question: "Given that anthropologists are generally prevented by the conditions under which they must work from employing the most powerful of the basic paradigms, the control-group paradigm, and are in fact sometimes restricted to using one of the weakest of these (the static group comparison), how can an anthropologist realistically hope to design and execute a study which will conclusively prove a hypothesis?"

The answer to this quite reasonable question is that he cannot. But, then, neither can a researcher in any field of science, for even the most powerful and sophisticated research designs are unable to eliminate completely all potential rival hypotheses.[1] A concept vital to understanding the nature of scientific research in anthropology, as in all fields, is that a study can only "probe" a hypothesis and can never "prove" it (Campbell and Stanley 1966:35). As Campbell and Stanley have noted (1966:36):

> Varying degrees of "confirmation" are conferred upon a theory through the number of *plausible rival hypotheses* available to account for the data. The fewer such plausible rival hypotheses remaining, the greater the degree of "confirmation." Presumably, at any stage of accumulation of evidence, even for the most advanced science, there are numerous possible theories compatible with the data, particularly if all theories involving complex contingencies be allowed. Yet for "well-established" theories, and theories thoroughly probed by complex experiments, few if any rivals may be practically available or seriously proposed.

While the research designs generally available to anthropologists are not as efficient as those used in some fields, they nonetheless can effectively *probe* hypotheses. No single study will eliminate all plausible rival hypotheses, especially if it must employ a weak paradigm, but by emphasizing *cumulative, complementary research* we can hope to attain a high degree of confirmation for specific hypotheses. By cumulative, complementary research is meant research in which the same hypothesis is tested in a variety of ways and in a variety of contexts, generally, but not necessarily, by different investigators. The importance of such an emphasis derives, as Campbell and Stanley again point out (1966:36), from the fact that:

> the more numerous and independent the ways in which . . . [an] effect is demonstrated, the less numerous and less plausible any singular rival invalidating hypothesis becomes. The appeal is to parsimony. . . . If several sets of differences can all be explained by the single hypothesis that X has an effect, while several separate uncontrolled-variable effects must be hypothesized, a different one for each observed difference, then the effect of X becomes the most tenable.

By stressing cumulative, complementary research we may then hope to attain high levels of confidence regarding many anthropological hypotheses, notwithstanding our frequent inability to employ the most powerful research paradigms.

The perspective on research design we have developed in this book has, we feel, implications for another issue we have not yet treated. This concerns the current debate in anthropology regarding the relative merits of the "emic" and "etic" approaches to the analysis of human behavior. The terms emic and etic derive from the linguistic terms "phonemic" and "phonetic" and have acquired broader application, primarily through analogic applications within anthropology, as a result of

---

[1] For example, the rival hypothesis of chance can only be discounted and never completely eliminated, even if the very powerful control-group paradigm is used.

the pioneering work of the linguist Kenneth Pike (1954–1960). In brief, the proponents of the emic view within anthropology hold that the concepts used and found meaningful by the native actors themselves will be more useful in the analysis of human behavior than will concepts and distinctions not meaningful to them. Eticists urge instead that scientific data be analyzed using concepts developed by scientific observers—concepts which are not necessarily meaningful to ordinary members of the culture being analyzed. From the perspective of hypothesis-testing research, this debate is easily resolved. The best strategy for analysis is clearly that which produces valid and useful hypotheses, regardless whether the concepts measured are emic or etic. We thus join Pelto (1970:85) in urging that anthropological researchers "adopt a free-wheeling pragmatism in [their] modes of categorizing cultural observations . . . since the only useful test of our classifications is in the successes and failures of our hypothesis testing and theory building."

Another major issue arising from the views presented in the previous chapters pertains broadly to the moral implications of this research strategy. As we noted in the introduction, hypothesis-testing research has recently become more common in anthropology as interest has shifted from description per se toward explanation. One concomitant of this trend has been an increased realization on the part of many anthropologists of the need to design research in a way that will ensure that one's tests of hypotheses are maximally effective. Some anthropologists, however, do not regard this new anthropological concern with research design as an entirely unmixed blessing. Some, indeed, view it with varying degrees of alarm. We believe that the opposition which has been voiced to increased emphasis on well-designed hypothesis-testing research in anthropology, while no doubt sincerely conceived and well intentioned, derives from an emotional rather than a logical basis, and that a careful analysis of the situation can leave little doubt that higher standards of research design will benefit the anthropological enterprise.

Nevertheless, we will examine carefully three arguments frequently raised against increased emphasis on research design in anthropology. One argument suggests that well-designed research necessarily brings with it a reluctance to deal with phenomena not amenable to powerful and efficient research designs. Thus, vital, relevant, but often less manageable phenomena—war, poverty, human happiness, and so forth—will tend to be avoided since they are unsuited to study by "elegant" means such as the "controlled experiment" (the control-group paradigm). A second and related argument suggests that an emphasis on rigorous research design, with its implied commitment to "scientific neutrality," will result in a decrease in civic commitment or involvement. A third argument is that an emphasis on well-designed research will contribute to the erosion of ethical standards, as there will be a strong tendency for the anthropologist committed to well-designed research to sacrifice ethical principles for the principles of research design.

All of these arguments assume that commitment to good research design and knowledge of research design principles will cause the anthropologist to regard elegance of research design as an end itself, to be valued above considerations of relevance, commitment, and ethics. This is a colossal non sequitur. A concern for good research design does not have to lead to the simple-minded pursuit of sterile elegance in the design of research. Rather, it can provide a sound basis for commitment through the conduct of relevant research that is within the dictates of one's ethical code. Let us briefly consider why this is the case by examining each of these arguments in a little more detail.

Relevance

The first argument suggests that an increased interest in the quality of one's research design will bring a reluctance to deal with vital, relevant human issues such as war, poverty, and human happiness. Relevance has unquestionably assumed a high priority among anthropologists. This can be seen in the many discussions and debates at anthropological conventions and in the numerous letters, articles, and reports that discuss the relevance of anthropological research. For example, Onwuachi and Wolfe (1966:95), in discussing current research in Africa, remind us that "if we, as anthropologists, are free to choose our own problems, then we must accept the responsibility for not having chosen to study the most relevant problems for the future." Armed with this undeniable premise, they continue by asserting that "if we insist on skirting controversial problems, relevant problems, and try to stay in . . . so-called traditional anthropological slots, we will have no place in the future of Africa or anywhere else." We would agree that without a shift in our research interests, there may be an end to the place of anthropologists and anthropological research in Africa and other parts of the world. But it is by no means clear that controversy is the best indicator of relevance. The demand that anthropologists conduct "relevant" research has become so clouded by the reality of controversy in our lives that many anthropologists seem willing to be satisfied that the profession is becoming more relevant simply because we talk about (and pass resolutions on) controversial issues. We would argue, however, that while such action can be useful, the real relevance of our discipline will be established as we systematically consider factors which can add to the explanatory power of our research. Then, when we study controversial issues, we will be able to make statements that are highly relevant.

Commitment

The desire to become more relevant is closely related to another interest—becoming commited to social or civic issues. In the midst of the social and political tumult of recent years, such concerns have taken on special importance for anthropologists. For many, any form of neutrality and detachment has become suspect. Moreover, it is often (and, we think, erroneously) assumed that an increased interest in the rigor of our research and an orientation toward hypothesis testing will result in excessive concern for being "neutral," with a corresponding decline in commitment to the pressing issues of the day. Some anthropologists see such neutrality, or any kind of neutrality, as the ultimate dehumanization of the most human of the sciences. This complex matter is made even more difficult by general confusion about the various kinds of neutrality that may be exhibited by a researcher. One form of neutrality is often recommended to help ensure that the results of an investigation will not simply reflect the points of view held by the investigator prior to the research. Another form of neutrality, often but erroneously seen as an extension of the previous form, is seen when individuals choose to remain uncommitted (neutral) on various issues, often including important social or political issues. This form of neutrality is seen by many as being particularly undesirable because it is felt that social scientists, by virtue of their special expertise, have an obligation to commit themselves one way or another on vital public issues. The rationale behind this position has been stated by Lynd (among others). He suggests (1939:186) that "either the social sciences know more than do *de facto* leaders of the culture as to what the findings of research mean, as to the options the institutional system presents, as to what human personalities want, why they want them, and how desirable changes can be effected, *or* the vast current industry of social sciences is an empty facade." In a similar vein, an anthropological colleague, Katherine Gough, has asked, "Who is to evaluate and suggest guidelines for human society, if not those who study it?" (quoted in Berreman 1968:394).

In America today, there are many who would answer Gough's question by asserting that anyone who lives life is at least as qualified to make suggestions for its betterment as the social scientists who study it. Others would decry this answer as anti-intellectualism at its worst. We would insist, however, that it is time for anthropologists to examine their efforts to date and seriously assess the extent to which it is justifiable to lay claim (implicitly or explicitly) to the label "expert." Few would dispute the right of persons to speak their minds on issues of interest to them, but many have objected to the speaking of one's "expert mind" when in fact there is serious doubt about the extent to which the views are truly expert. The fact that a piece of "relevant" research has been done by a researcher who is "committed" is not sufficient grounds for viewing the research as expertly done (or the recommendations which derive from it as valid). It seems quite likely that much of what anthropologists claim to "know" is questionable at least on the grounds of faulty research designs and that rather than contributing to knowledge these erroneous views only serve to reinforce the widespread notion that the vast industry of social science is an "empty façade" (for an interesting and polemical discussion which takes such a view, see Andreski 1972). Thus, rather than fostering a desire for neutrality and noncommitment, a balanced interest in rigorous research design is an essential prerequisite for sound professional commitment to important social issues.

Ethics

The third argument we will consider suggests that an emphasis on research design will contribute to the erosion of ethical standards because the anthropologist committed to well-designed research will sacrifice ethical principles in favor of these methodological ones. There is, indeed, considerable interest in the ethical side of anthropological research today. Informant rights, relations with colleagues, with our government, and with the governments of host countries, the nature of our research goals, the sources of our funding—these and many other issues of vital concern to *all* anthropologists are being widely discussed and debated. The dilemma posed by the assumption that the demands of "science" and one's ethical principles are incompatible is, therefore, a most serious one. It is in this context that we have the chilling visions of anthropological Dr. Strangeloves blitzkrieging their way over humanity in search of "scientific truth." However, to assume that such foreboding trends will spring directly from increased concern for rigorous research seems to rest on an unduly negative view of anthropologists.

It is true, of course, that anthropologists will find it difficult to conduct research —whether rigorously designed or not—which, by all normative systems, could be judged to have exacted no ethical costs of any kind. The very presence of an anthropologist in the field collecting data, or the very act of making information about people public (through teaching and publishing) implies that some people are, or have been in the past, giving up time, money, privacy, and even safety in a way which would not have happened had the anthropologist not conducted his research. Consequently, ethical guidelines that call for the anthropologist to completely avoid harming persons who are the object of research, or to totally guarantee their privacy, cannot, in the real world of research, ever be achieved. The ethical issues that inevitably will have to be faced, then—regardless of the rigor of one's research—must be understood as matters of degree. It is not a matter of "invading privacy or not," or "harming informants indirectly by publishing or not." Rather, it is "To what degree will publishing the results of one's research be harmful to the informants?" and "To what degree will the privacy of individuals be invaded?"

Thus, although there are many potentially valuable ethical principles to be considered, it is by no means the case that a concern for rigorous research design will result in their being ignored. In fact, living up to what we believe to be one of the most fundamental ethical obligations is actually facilitated—not hindered—by an increased concern for sound research design. That is, one of the most serious threats to the integrity of the anthropological profession, from the standpoint of ethics, comes not from increasing dedication to well-designed research but from failing to recognize the ethical implications of giving advice or becoming committed on the basis of results obtained through poorly designed research. For some, rigorous research is unethical research because it is expected that ethics will be sacrificed for rigor. For us, *unsound research is unethical research* because erroneous views may be accepted as factual by the unwary. Clearly, such a situation is unacceptable, for as Jorgensen has noted (1971:332–333):

> *we have an ethical obligation to withhold our research reports until we know what we have.* I do not expect the study of anthropology to become a rigorous inductive undertaking overnight, nor do I think all wrong guesses in our explanations are unethical. Quite to the contrary, I think we can learn from our mistakes. But our mistakes can become more and more costly to our informants as the conditions under which we and they operate change. Thus, I think *we have an obligation to make systematic comparisons and exercise systematic controls in our research to ensure that our generalizations are valid.* That is the least we can expect of ourselves and our colleagues when we realize that policy can be formulated on the basis of our research reports [italics added].

And so, for a third time, we can see that a balanced concern for the adequacy of our research design does not lead inextricably to the dire results often predicted. Rather, such concerns can give us the basis for achieving a more ethical science.

Summary

It is essential that we all maintain a reasonable perspective about the accomplishments and potentials of contemporary anthropology as a discipline capable of providing solutions to basic social and political problems. Anthropologists are, by and large, sensitive and concerned citizens of their respective countries, and they do focus their professional lives on the sociocultural aspects of the world at large. It is not surprising then, that many suggestions regarding social problems have emerged from this group of professionals which have been seen as helpful, insightful, and adoptable. But one should not, on these grounds alone, take this as evidence of the high state of the art of anthropological research.

The relatively voluminous literature in applied anthropology attests to the interest anthropologists have in putting their knowledge to the acid test of practical work for the betterment of mankind. But this same literature also attests to the rather considerable difficulties faced and the disappointments and failures encountered—often, in fact, because the research was poorly designed. Beals, in noting the disastrous results that ensued after anthropologists contributed to the writing of certain laws pertaining to American Indians, provides a case in point. Here the experience was so disappointing that Beals was prompted to suggest that "many United States anthropologists came to doubt whether knowledge of culture and society was adequate to proposing major solutions to social issues ..." (1968:407).[2]

For some, the case for pessimism about the potential of anthropology can occasionally appear overwhelming, and seems to argue for a neutrality that comes from impotence. We, however, remain optimistic that by utilizing sound research design, anthropology can meaningfully contribute to the solution of mankind's problems. Moreover, we would support those who raise the fundamental humanist question: "Knowledge for what?" Anthropologists do not work in a vacuum and they do not have the privilege (if that is what it would be) of ignoring the implications of their work. Gough (1968:429) fears we shall, if we ignore the basic humanist question, "lapse into disconnected trivialities, insignificant or even harmful makework, and alienating mental exercises." While we would question whether it is possible for most research to be neatly typed as trivial makework or its presumed opposite, it is nonetheless important to recognize that much effort can be expended on trivial exercises when, for similar efforts using similar anthropological skills, effort may be directed to issues representing clear and present needs. To the extent that we as anthropologists, a group of professionals committed to the betterment of man's condition, have shirked our responsibilities in this way, then to that extent, we have misdirected our energies.

---

[2] It must be emphasized that many so-called "experts" make truly monumental and disastrous errors. Indeed, this is often most dramatically the case in fields with older and more established traditions which favor the use of rigorous, elaborately designed research. The experiences in recent years in such diverse fields as urban planning, ecology, psychology, medicine, economics, and education are tragically illustrative. What the experiences in these fields demonstrate and what anthropologists must remember as a consequence, is that the application of the fruits of well designed research is more an art than a science. Moreover, they remind us that the mere fact that a piece of research has been conducted rigorously provides no guarantee whatsoever that the application of the resulting "knowledge" will be either fruitful or morally justifiable. Nevertheless, the fact that the application of knowledge is primarily an art provides no justification for the continued use of weak methods when stronger ones are feasible, for to do so only compounds the difficulties.

All of this leads us to the general conclusion that if anthropology is to play a more active role in the vital issues confronting mankind today, one of our first concerns will have to be the improvement of the methods through which we come to understand human behavior. For as Marvin Harris has recently observed (1971: 330), ". . . the task of anthropology is to understand the world first and to change it second. To make understanding the slave of action is contrary to our professional understanding of the relationship between theory and practice." In a word, the urgent need is to increase the ability of anthropologists to do research more rigorously so they will be in a better position to make the kinds of socially and personally relevant contributions to knowledge that are so desperately needed.

References

ANDRESKI, S., 1972, *Social Sciences as Sorcery.* London: Andre Deutsch.

BARKER, R. G., and H. WRIGHT, 1951, *One Boy's Day.* New York: Harper & Row.

——, 1954, *Midwest and Its Children.* New York: Row, Peterson.

BARRY, H., III, I. L. CHILD, and M. K. BACON, 1959, Relation of Child Training to Subsistence Economy. *American Anthropologist* 61:51–63.

BEALS, R., 1968, Comments on: Social Responsibilities Symposium. *Current Anthropology* 9:407–408.

BEATTIE, J., 1965, *Understanding an African Kingdom: Bunyoro.* New York: Holt, Rinehart and Winston.

BERELSON, B. and R. FREEDMAN, 1964, A Study in Fertility Control. *Scientific American* 210(5):29–37.

BERREMAN, G. D., 1962, *Behind Many Masks: Ethnography and Impression Management in a Himalayan Village.* Ithaca, New York: Society for Applied Anthropology, Monograph #4.

——, 1968, Is Anthropology Alive? Social Responsibility in Social Anthropology. *Current Anthropology* 9:391–396.

BIRDWHISTELL, R. L., 1970, *Kinesics and Context: Essays on Body Motion Communication.* Philadelphia: Pennsylvania University Press.

BLALOCK, H. M., 1964, *Causal Inferences in Nonexperimental Research.* New York: Norton.

——, 1972, *Social Statistics.* New York: McGraw-Hill.

BLALOCK, H. M., and A. B. BLALOCK (Eds.), 1968, *Methodology in Social Research.* New York: McGraw-Hill.

BRIM, J. A., 1970, *Local Systems and Modernizing Change in the New Territories of Hong Kong.* Ph.D. Dissertation, Stanford University.

CAMPBELL, D. T., and J. C. STANLEY, 1966, *Experimental and Quasi-experimental Designs for Research.* Chicago: Rand McNally.

CHURCHMAN, C. W., and P. RATOOSH, 1959, *Measurement: Definition and Theories.* New York: Wiley.

COCHRAN, W. G., 1953, *Sampling Techniques.* New York: Wiley.

COCHRAN, W. G., and G. M. COX, 1957, *Experimental Designs.* New York: Wiley.

COHEN, R., 1973, Selecting Respondents for a Study of Divorce in Nigeria. In W. M. O'Barr, M. A. Tessler, and D. H. Spain (Eds.), *Survey Research in Africa: Its Applications and Limits.* Evanston, Illinois: Northwestern University Press.

COHEN, R., L. L. LANGNESS, J. MIDDLETON, V. C. UCHENDU, and J. W. VANSTONE, 1970, Entree into the Field. In R. Naroll and R. Cohen (Eds.), *A Handbook of Method in Cultural Anthropology.* New York: Natural History Press.

COLE, M., J. GAY, J. A. GLICK, and D. W. SHARP, 1971, *The Cultural Context of Learning and Thinking.* New York: Basic Books.

CRONBACH, L. J., 1967, Coefficient Alpha and the Internal Structure of Tests. In W. A. Mehrens and R. L. Ebel (Eds.), *Principles of Educational and Psychological Measurement.* Chicago: Rand McNally.

EDWARDS, A. L., 1960, *Experimental Design in Psychological Research.* New York: Holt, Rinehart and Winston.

EGGAN, F., 1954, Social Anthropology and the Method of Controlled Comparison. *American Anthropologist* 56:743–760.

EVANS-PRITCHARD, E. E., 1963, *The Comparative Method in Social Anthropology.* London: Athlone.

114   REFERENCES

EYSENCK, H. J., and D. B. PRELL, 1951, The Inheritance of Neuroticism: An Experimental Study. *Journal of Mental Science* 97:441–465.

FESTINGER, L. and D. KATZ (Eds.), 1953, *Research Methods in the Behavioral Sciences*. New York: Holt, Rinehart and Winston.

FESTINGER, L., and H. H. KELLEY, 1951, *Changing Attitudes through Social Contact*. Ann Arbor: Research Center for Group Dynamics, Institute for Social Research.

FREEDMAN, R. F., and J. Y. TAKESHITA, 1969, *Family Planning in Taiwan*. Princeton, N.J.: Princeton University Press.

FREILICH, M. (Ed.), 1970, *Marginal Natives: Anthropologists at Work*. New York: Harper & Row.

FREY, F. W., 1969, *Survey Research on Comparative Social Change: A Bibliography*. Cambridge, Mass.: M.I.T. Press.

GISELLI, E. E., 1964, *Theory of Psychological Measurement*. New York: McGraw-Hill.

GLOCK, C. Y. (Ed.), 1967, *Survey Research in the Social Sciences*. New York: Russell Sage Foundation.

GOUGH, K., 1968, New Proposals for Anthropologists. *Current Anthropology* 9:403–407.

HANSEN, M. H., W. N. HURWITZ, and W. G. MADOW, 1953, *Sample Survey Methods and Theory*. New York: Wiley.

HARDYCK, C. D., and L. F. PETRINOVICH, 1969, *Introduction to Statistics for the Behavioral Sciences*. Philadelphia: Saunders.

HARRIS, M., 1968, *The Rise of Anthropological Theory*. New York: Crowell.

———, 1971, Review of: C. Valentine, Culture and Poverty: Critique and Counterproposals. *American Anthropologist* 73:330–331.

HAYS, W. L., 1965, *Statistics for Psychologists*. New York: Holt, Rinehart and Winston.

JONGMANS, D. C., and P. W. C. GUTKIND, 1967, *Anthropologists in the Field*. Assen: Van Gorcum.

JORGENSEN, J. G., 1971, On Ethics and Anthropology. *Current Anthropology* 12:321–334.

KAPLAN, A., 1964, *The Conduct of Inquiry: Methodology for Behavioral Science*. San Francisco: Chandler.

KIRK, R. E., 1968, *Experimental Design: Procedures for the Behavioral Sciences*. Belmont, California: Brooks/Cole.

KISH, L., 1965, *Survey Sampling*. New York: Wiley.

LAZARSFELD, P. F., and M. ROSENBERG (Eds.), 1955, *The Language of Social Research: A Reader in the Methodology of Social Research*. New York: Free Press.

LEFKOWITZ, M. M., R. R. BLAKE, and J. S. MOUTON, 1955, Status Factors in Pedestrian Violation of Traffic Signals. *Journal of Abnormal and Social Psychology* 51:704–706.

LEVINE, R. A., 1966, *Dreams and Deeds: Achievement Motivation in Nigeria*. Chicago: University of Chicago Press.

LINDQUIST, E. F., 1953, *Design and Analysis of Experiments in Psychology and Education*. Boston: Houghton Mifflin.

LYND, R., 1949, *Knowledge for What?* Princeton: Princeton University Press.

MCCLELLAND, D. C., 1961, *The Achieving Society*. Princeton: Van Nostrand.

———, J. W. ATKINSON, R. A. CLARK, and E. L. LOWELL, 1953, *The Achievement Motive*. New York: Appleton-Century-Crofts.

———, and D. G. WINTER, 1969, *Motivating Economic Achievement*. New York: The Free Press.

MCEWEN, W. J., 1963, Forms and Problems of Validation in Social Anthropology. *Current Anthropology* 4:155–183.

MEAD, M., 1949, *Coming of Age in Samoa*. New York: Mentor. (First published in 1928.)

————, 1972, *Blackberry Winter: My Earlier Years*. New York: Morrow.

MEHRENS, W. A., and R. L. EBEL, 1967, *Principles of Educational and Psychological Measurement*. Chicago: Rand McNally.

MILLER, D. C., 1964, *Handbook of Research Design and Social Measurement*. New York: McKay.

MISCHEL, W., 1961, Father-absence and Delay of Gratification. *Journal of Abnormal and Social Psychology* 63:116–124.

MOSER, C.A., and G. KALTON, 1972, *Survey Methods in Social Investigation*. New York: Basic Books.

MOSIER, C. I., 1967, A Critical Examination of the Concepts of Face Validity. In W. A. Mehrens and R. L. Ebel (Eds.), *Principles of Educational and Psychological Measurement*. Chicago: Rand McNally.

MUESSLER, J. H., K. F. SCHUESSLER, and H. L. COSTNER, 1970, *Statistical Reasoning in Sociology*. (2nd ed.) Boston: Houghton Mifflin.

NADEL, S. F., 1952, Witchcraft in Four African Societies: An Essay in Comparison. *American Anthropologist* 54:18–29.

NAROLL, R., 1962, *Data Quality Control: A New Research Technique*. New York: Free Press.

————, and R. COHEN (Eds.), 1970, *A Handbook of Method in Cultural Anthropology*. New York: Natural History Press.

NUNNALLY, J. C., 1967, *Psychometric Theory*. New York: McGraw-Hill.

O'BARR, W. M., D. H. SPAIN, and M. A. TESSLER (Eds.), 1973, *Survey Research in Africa: Its Applications and Limits*. Evanston, Ill.: Northwestern University Press.

OTTERBEIN, K. F., 1969, Basic Steps in Conducting a Cross-cultural Study. *Behavior Science Notes* 4:221–236.

ONWUACHI, P. C., and A. W. WOLFE, 1966, The Place of Anthropology in the Future of Africa. *Human Organization* 25:93–95.

PARSONS, T., 1966, *Societies: Evolutionary and Comparative Perspectives*. Englewood Cliffs, N.J.: Prentice-Hall.

PELTO, P. J., 1970, *Anthropological Research: The Structure of Inquiry*. New York: Harper & Row.

PIKE, K., 1954–1960, *Language in Relation to a Unified Theory of the Structures of Human Behavior*. Glendale, Cal.: Summer Institute of Linguistics.

ROBINSON, J. P., and P. R. SHAVER, 1969, *Measures of Social Psychological Attitudes*. Ann Arbor, Mich.: Institute for Social Research, University of Michigan.

ROYAL ANTHROPOLOGICAL INSTITUTE, 1951, *Notes and Queries on Anthropology*. (6th ed.) London: Routledge.

ROHNER, R. P., n.d., *The Cross-cultural Method*. New York: Holt, Rinehart and Winston. (In preparation.)

ROKKAN, S., S. VERBA, J. VIET, and E. ALMASY, 1969, *Comparative Survey Analysis*. Paris: Mouton.

ROSENTHAL, R., 1966, *Experimenter Effects in Behavioral Research*. New York: Appleton-Century-Crofts.

RUDNER, R. S., 1966, *Philosophy of Social Science*. Englewood Cliffs, N.J.: Prentice-Hall.

SCHUESSLER, K., 1973, *Sampling in Social Research*. Englewood Cliffs, N.J.: Prentice-Hall.

SENDERS, V. L., 1958, *Measurement and Statistics*. New York: Oxford University Press.

SPAIN, D. H., 1973, Developing a New TAT for Studying Achievement Motivation in Africa. In W. M. O'Barr, D. H. Spain, and M. A. Tessler (Eds.), *Survey Research in Africa: Its Applications and Limits*. Evanston, Ill.: Northwestern University Press.

SPINDLER, G. D. (Ed.), 1970, *Being an Anthropologist: Fieldwork in Eleven Cultures*. New York: Holt, Rinehart and Winston.

STOUFFER, S. A., ET AL., 1950, *Measurement and Prediction*. Princeton: Princeton University Press.

SUCHMAN, E., A. CEBOLLERO, R. MUNOZ, and D. O. PABON, 1967, An Experiment in Innovation among Sugar Cutters in Puerto Rico. *Human Organization* 26(4):214–221.

TAKESHITA, J. Y., 1966, Lessons Learned from Family Planning Studies in Taiwan and Korea. In B. Berelson et al. (Eds.), *Family Planning and Population Programs*. Chicago: University of Chicago Press.

THORNDIKE, R. L., 1942, Regression Fallacies in the Matched Groups Experiment. *Psychometrika* 7:85–102.

TYLOR, E. B., 1889, On a Method of Investigating the Development of Institutions; Applied to Laws of Marriage and Descent. *Journal of the Royal Anthropological Institute of Great Britain and Ireland* 18:245–272. (Reprinted in F. W. Moore [Ed.], *Readings in Cross-cultural Methodology*. New Haven: HRAF Press, 1961.)

WALLACE, A. F. C., 1970, *Culture and Personality*. (2nd ed.) New York: Random House.

WEBB, E. J., D. T. CAMPBELL, R. D. SCHWARTZ, and L. SECHREST, 1966, *Unobtrusive Measures: Non-reactive Research in the Social Sciences*. Chicago: Rand McNally.

WESTERMARCK, E. A., 1926, *A Short History of Marriage*. New York: Macmillan.

WHITING, B. B., ET AL. (Eds.), 1963, *Six Cultures: Studies of Child Rearing*. New York: Wiley.

WHITING, J. W. M., and I. L. CHILD, 1953, *Child Training and Personality: A Cross-cultural Study*. New Haven: Yale University Press.

WHITING, J. W. M., ET AL., 1954, *Field Guide for a Study of Socialization*. Cambridge, Mass.: Laboratory of Human Development, Mimeo. (Also vol. I of the Six Cultures Series, New York: Wiley, 1966.)

WILLIAMS, T. R., 1967, *Field Methods in the Study of Culture*. New York: Holt, Rinehart and Winston.

WINCH, R. F., and D. T. CAMPBELL, 1969, Proof? No. Evidence? Yes. The Significance of Tests of Significance. *American Sociologist* 4:140–143.

WOLF, A. P., 1970, Childhood Association and Sexual Attraction: A Further Test of the Westermarck Hypothesis. *American Anthropologist* 72:503–515.

Recommended Readings

Our principal goal in this list of recommended readings has been to provide a wide range of sources offering a variety of perspectives on the issues discussed in this book. We have assumed that the other books in the series in which this one appears are known to the reader, as are most of the items cited in the text and listed in the References. We have therefore limited our list to a few items in each of three broad categories: (1) basic works on design and methodology in anthropology and related social sciences; (2) works dealing with techniques, pragmatics, ethics, and the subjective nature of the fieldwork experience; and (3) books offering contrasting viewpoints about social science methodologies. The latter somewhat unorthodox category is provided on the premise that there is value in students becoming aware of the rather wide array of opinions on methodology that exists within the social sciences. Although we obviously do not share many of the viewpoints expressed by the authors of these books, we are convinced the reader will find the views interesting and provocative.

Basic works on design and methodology

CAMPBELL, D. T., and J. C. STANLEY, 1966, *Experimental and Quasi-experimental Designs for Research.* Chicago: Rand McNally. We have cited the authors of this excellent book throughout the text and have followed their lead in numerous ways. The reader who has found what we have said to be interesting cannot help but be interested in this more advanced treatment of research methodology.

KAPLAN, A. K., 1964, *The Conduct of Inquiry: Methodology for Behavior Science.* San Francisco: Chandler. A thorough discussion of the philosophy and methods of social science. It is a classic statement of great clarity, scope, and sophistication.

NAROLL, R. and R. COHEN (Eds.), 1970, *A Handbook of Method in Cultural Anthropology.* New York: Natural History Press. This encyclopedic survey of anthropological methods is a must for the serious student of research methods and techniques. The numerous contributors discuss a surprising array of issues, often with great sophistication and in considerable depth.

NUNNALLY, J. C., 1967, *Psychometric Theory.* New York: McGraw-Hill. An advanced treatment of measurement from a psychological perspective, but it is to be recommended as a brilliantly clear book which can offer a great deal to the creative anthropologist.

Works dealing with techniques, pragmatics, ethics, and the subjective nature of the fieldwork experience

BEALS, R. L., 1969, *Politics of Social Research: An Inquiry into the Ethics and Responsibilities of Social Scientists.* Chicago: Aldine. Although this book confronts ethical problems relevant to all the social sciences, the author, himself an anthropologist, focuses on issues of special significance to his immediate colleagues. Stimulated by "Project Camelot" and by the "Children of Sanchez Affair," it is essential reading for anyone contemplating fieldwork today.

SPINDLER, G. D., 1970, *Being an Anthropologist: Fieldwork in Eleven Cultures.*

New York: Holt, Rinehart and Winston. A rich source of insight into the nature of anthropological field research. Thirteen prominent anthropologists discuss problems they encountered in the conduct of field studies and describe their personal adaptations to specific field situations.

PELTO, P. J., 1970, *Anthropological Research: The Structure of Inquiry.* New York: Harper & Row. An introductory survey of anthropological research methods and techniques, covering a wide variety of important issues.

WATSON, J. B., and S. T. KIMBELL (Eds.), 1972, *Crossing Cultural Boundaries: The Anthropological Experience.* San Francisco: Chandler. An excellent collection of insightful personal statements about the nature of anthropological fieldwork. The contributors are among the most eminent of our colleagues, and the experiences they relate illustrate many important philosophical, ethical, and pragmatic points.

Books offering contrasting viewpoints about social science methodologies

ANDRESKI, S., 1972, *Social Sciences as Sorcery.* London: Andre Deutsch. The author describes the "mumbo-jumbo" jargon of the social sciences, arguing in his polemical style that social scientists with mediocre minds are trying to hide behind needless quantification, spineless objectivity, and smoke screens of jargon.

BECKER, E., 1971, *The Lost Science of Man.* New York: Braziller. A scholarly critique of American social science in general and American sociology and anthropology in particular through a review of the work of Albion Small (sociology) and Franz Boas (and many of his successors in anthropology). Becker argues that a shift away from a focus on larger issues toward an interest in more "scientific" problems and methods has weakened these social sciences.

DEVEREUX, G., 1967, *From Anxiety to Method in the Behavioral Sciences.* The Hague: Mouton. A complex and somewhat disorganized book which presents the interesting idea that anthropological fieldwork (as well as research of other social sciences) is as much an opportunity to learn about oneself as it is a chance to learn about others. Moreover, it is argued, the tendency to ignore this fact has been a detriment which can be overcome by the application of the psychoanalytic perspective to both fieldwork and fieldworker.